Jutland to Junkyard

Jutland to Junkyard

*The raising of the scuttled German
High Seas Fleet from Scapa Flow
– the greatest salvage operation of all time*

S.C. George

Birlinn

This edition published 1999 by
Birlinn Limited
Unit 8
Canongate Venture
5 New Street
Edinburgh EH8 8BH

First published in 1973 by Patrick Stephen Ltd

© Birlinn Ltd

ISBN 1 84158 001 5

British Library Cataloguing-in-Publication Data

A catalogue record for this book is available
from the British Library

Typeset in New Baskerville by Brinnoven, Livingston
Printed and bound in Finland by WSOY

Contents

Foreword

Rod MacDonald

Scapa Flow is a dramatic and windswept expanse of water some 12 miles across and almost completely encircled by the islands of Orkney. For centuries it has been a safe, sheltered and heavily defended anchorage for the Royal Navy. Great warships have come and gone. Dramatic deeds are an integral part of its past. Countless military man hours have gone into defensive planning and endeavour to render this great naval anchorage safe and impregnable to our wartime enemies. Those enemies in turn have gone to similar lengths in attempting to find a way through those defences to attack valuable Allied shipping.

Even today, more than half a century after the end of World War II, all around the sea passages into the Flow empty gun emplacements and barracks bear silent witness to its wartime role. In the dark depths of Scapa Flow lie countless testaments to man's inhumanity to man. U-boats attempting to penetrate into the Flow to attack Allied shipping were depth charged, or sunk by a controlled mine explosion after the sound of their engines had been picked up by detector cables laid across the seabed. Countless other vessels have come to grief in the Flow. Others have been sunk deliberately in attempts to block the minor sea passages. The seabed is littered with the legacy of its maritime past.

One U-boat, *U47* under the command of Lieut. Cmdr. Günther Prien, did manage to slip past the British defences on 14 October 1939 in the dead of night and torpedo the 29,000-ton British battleship HMS *Royal Oak* at anchor. *Royal Oak* turned turtle within five minutes and sank in 30 metres of water with her crew still trapped inside her. The torpedo explosions destroyed her power circuits and the whole ship below decks was pitched into darkness. Crew members stumbled around desperately in the darkness, groping for a way out of her labyrinthine insides as *Royal Oak* keeled over. In all, 833 officers and men died in that one attack. The 19,560-ton British battleship HMS *Vanguard* was destroyed in a single cataclysmic magazine explosion on 9 July 1917 with the loss of more than 700 men.

Scapa Flow is however probably best known nowadays as the final resting place of the remains of the German Imperial Navy's High Seas Fleet of World War I. The High Seas Fleet had been interned at Scapa Flow in November 1918 as a condition of the armistice which suspended the hostilities pending peace negotiations which would eventually lead to the Treaty of Versailles. Fearing that those negotiations were about to break down and that the British would seize the Fleet, Rear Admiral Ludwig von Reuter gave the order on 21 June 1919 to scuttle it. All 74 warships of the fleet, giant battle cruisers, battleships, light cruisers and torpedo boat destroyers scuttled simultaneously and sank to the bottom of Scapa Flow. It was and still is the single greatest act of maritime suicide the world has ever seen.

Initially the British Admiralty resolved to leave the sunken fleet to rust on the bottom of Scapa Flow for ever. By the 1920s however the price of scrap metal, initially so abundant and cheap at the end of the Great War, had picked up and the salvagers' attentions turned to the seemingly endless supply of high quality German scrap metal lying on the seabed. Additionally the sunken warships, some only partially submerged, had proved to be a hazard to navigation with a number of other vessels running aground on them. Over the coming decades the majority of the 74 warships were raised intact from the depths in a mammoth, ground-breaking salvage operation.

The last vessel of the High Seas Fleet to be raised intact from the seabed was the 26,180-ton battle cruiser *Derfflinger*, brought to the surface in 1939 from a record depth of 45 metres. She was towed to Rosyth for breaking but the outbreak of World War II led to the Admiralty taking over control of the dry dock where the vessel would have been broken down. *Derfflinger* lay at Rosyth throughout the war and was finally broken down in 1946.

All bar seven of the High Seas Fleet had been salvaged during these decades of incredible marine salvage. The 26,000-ton battleships *Kronprinz Wilhelm*, *Markgraf* and *König* all lay in deep water of between 35 and 45 metres with awkward lists of 30 to 40 degrees, settling year by year into the clinging mud of the seabed. The smaller 5,500-ton light cruisers *Cöln*, *Karlsruhe*, *Brummer* and *Dresden*, all lay on their sides in relatively deep water. They would be difficult wrecks to raise from the seabed and did not hold sufficient of worth to merit salvage. The salvors therefore abandoned any attempts to raise these seven vessels whole. Over the succeeding years some small-scale salvaging of the remaining vessels of the High Seas Fleet was carried out mainly by the use of explosives to blast open the engine room areas and remove the valuable non-ferrous engine machinery. That having been done the seven ghosts of the High Seas fleet were left to lie in peace on the seabed.

Jutland to Junkyard is thus a fascinating account of these times, the dramatic scuttling and the momentous salvage works in the following decades by charismatic characters. In writing the book, S.C. George went to painstaking lengths to trace and interview the actual characters involved in the work. It is based on genuine firsthand accounts and is full of fascinating anecdotes from the actual people involved. If he had not gone to these lengths and recorded these memories for future generations they would have passed into oblivion. Now they are here for posterity, for all of us interested in the subject to learn from.

When *Jutland to Junkyard* was published in 1973, S.C. George probably thought that the remaining seven vessels would be left in the dark depths of Scapa Flow to rust away to nothing in ignominy, passing silently into the history books and of little interest to future generations. Whereas the focus of the world's attention had been on Scapa Flow at the time of the momentous salvage attempts in the 1930s, not much interest was being shown in the remaining vessels on the seabed. In the years following its publication however, there has been a huge surge in the popularity of scuba diving. Progressively throughout the 1970s more and more divers started visiting Scapa Flow enticed by the legend of the scuttling, the momentous salvage works and the ghost ships lying on the bottom. Each wreck is a time capsule that represents an era of sea power and majesty that has long since passed into the history books. Scapa Flow became a place of pilgrimage for divers eager to visit these huge relics of a distant war and the countless other wrecks that have come to grief there and litter the seabed.

Scapa Flow in 1973 had only very limited facilities for visiting divers. Divers had to be robust and ingenious to find and dive the wrecks. Quite often they would have to take their own compressor to Orkney to fill air tanks, along with their own inflatable boat to get out to the wreck sites. Some divers camped ashore. The wrecks were not buoyed and the navigational aids that divers use nowadays were not around. Divers had a compass, a set of transits and a depth sounder at best and had to search the wide expanse of the Flow themselves to find the wrecks. There were no dive charter vessels to take divers out to the wreck sites.

Over the years as more divers came north to the Flow the commercial potential of the German World War I wrecks became appreciated and in the late 1970s the first hard boat charters started up, taking parties of up to 12 divers at a time out to explore the wrecks. Progressively more dive charter businesses set up and nowadays there are usually about 10 to 15 dive charter boats working the Flow. In the good diving months of the year here, between April and October, most of these boats will have their full complement of 12 divers aboard diving six days a week. Some of the boats now offer a liveaboard package. A recent innovation has been the start up of a venture designed to reveal the secrets of the Flow to non divers via the use of a Remotely Operated Vehicle (ROV). This is an agile underwater camera used extensively in the offshore oil industry, which can be remotely 'flown' over the wreck by operators in a passenger-carrying boat above. The ROV sends live footage as it navigates around the wreck up to TV screens on the boat above enabling the passengers to share in the excitement of exploring one of the famous wrecks. In all, thousands of divers visit Orkney each year bringing much appreciated revenue to local businesses, dive/souvenir shops, hotels and pubs and not just to the dive charter boats themselves. Groups of divers make trips here from the USA and Europe, and in diving circles Scapa

Flow is known and revered internationally as one of the great dive locations of the world. The value of the income to Orkney from the wrecks of Scapa Flow cannot be underestimated.

When I was researching material for my own book *Dive Scapa Flow* in 1989, *Jutland to Junkyard* was one of my main reference books. I didn't have a copy myself and it proved very difficult to get hold of it through my local library as it was long out of print. As far as I am aware it was only reprinted once, in 1981. I am therefore very pleased to see this essential book published again and once more on the shelves of bookshops and libraries in Orkney and on the mainland. It is part of Orkney's heritage. New generations of divers and non divers alike can now rediscover a fascinating chapter of Scapa Flow's rich maritime history.

Rod Macdonald,
February 1999

Illustrations

Illustrations

MAPS AND FIGURES

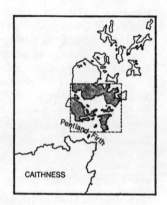

*Map of Scapa Flow and
surrounding area.*

CAITHNESS

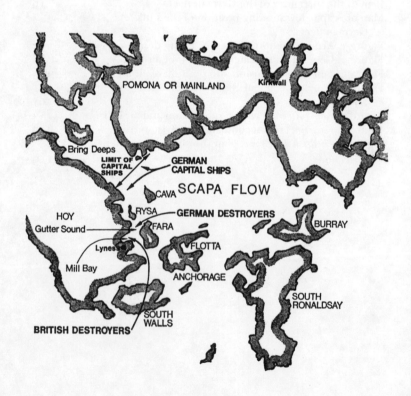

POMONA OR MAINLAND   Kirkwall

Bring Deeps

LIMIT OF
CAPITAL
SHIPS   GERMAN
               CAPITAL SHIPS

CAVA   SCAPA FLOW

RYSA   GERMAN DESTROYERS

HOY
Gutter Sound   FARA   BURRAY

Lyness

Mill Bay   FLOTTA

ANCHORAGE

                                SOUTH
                                RONALDSAY

          SOUTH
          WALLS
BRITISH DESTROYERS

1

The Storm Clouds Gather

THE GERMAN EMPIRE WAS born after the humiliation of France in the Franco-Prussian War of 1870. Germany's power-potential ran with her ambition. Towards the end of the decade she watched France, Russia and Italy begin to modernise and expand their navies, then herself became a competitor in the arms race.

At first, Germany regarded France and Russia as her most dangerous rivals. As her industrial and military growth increased and as she participated in the European scramble for land in Africa, England watched her with increasing misgiving, especially when in 1898 Germany's first Navy Law was passed and the strength of her fleet fixed at:

19 battleships (two in reserve);
8 armoured coast defence ships;
6 large cruisers;
16 smaller cruisers and, for foreign service, 6 large and 14 smaller, cruisers.

Then Germany began a naval building programme intended to break Britain's grip on European waters. The German Naval Bill of 1900 stated: 'Germany must have a battle fleet so strong that even the adversary possessed of the greatest sea power will attack it only with grave risk to herself'. The Kaiser supported Tirpitz to whom he said that 'with every new German battleship there was laid down a fresh pledge for peace the golden'. Germany was convinced that she had every right to build ships for the protection of her new colonies and her sea-borne trade.

In 1902 British anxieties were aggravated by the unintentional disclosure of German plans to build even more heavy ships, while a study of plans of the battleships disclosed all too clearly that they were intended to provide a short-range striking-force. Her navy was based mainly at Kiel and Wilhelmshaven, two convenient sites for rapid entry into the North Sea.

In 1906 Britain secretly built a new type of battleship, the *Dreadnought*, whose armament was all of the same calibre. This class of ship had ten 12-inch guns mounted in five twin-turrets. Four of these guns could be trained in the same direction, which enabled them to fire a broadside two-and-a-half times heavier than had previously been possible. Displacement was doubled to 18,000 tons to enable better armoured protection to be provided, and speed was 21.5 knots. Two years later a battle-cruiser was brought into service with 12-inch guns mounted in four twin-turrets and, as these could all be trained in the same direction, their broadside equalled that of the *Dreadnought*'s, while their speed of 26 knots rivalled that of the fastest cruisers.

In 1907 the German Reichstag passed a vast naval construction bill. The programme was to be completed by 1917. Besides battleships and torpedo craft it included 38 small cruisers. Larger dry-docks were built and the Kiel Canal was widened.

Germany's programme of reconstruction started with the *Nassau* class of ship armed with 12 11-inch guns and 12 5.9-inch guns. Succeeding classes were equal both in size and power to contemporary British ships. These classes were: *Helgoland* (four ships), *Kaiser* (five ships), *König* (four ships) and *Bayern* (three ships). The first three classes, armed with 12-inch guns, had speeds of 20 to 21 knots; the last class carried eight 15-inch guns and had speeds of 23 to 24 knots. All ships had a secondary armament of 12 to 16 5.9-inch guns. The first of the series of battleships was *Blücher*, 15,500 tons displacement, speed 24 knots, armed with 12 8.2-inch, eight 5.9-inch and six 3.4-inch guns and four 18-inch torpedoes. This was followed by *von der Tann, Moltke, Goeben, Seydlitz, Derfflinger, Lützow* and *Hindenburg*.

About three light cruisers were built each year ranging from the *Dresden* class with a displacement of 3,650 tons and a speed of 24 knots to the *Königsberg* class with a displacement of 5,600 tons and a speed of $27\frac{1}{2}$ knots.

At the beginning of the 20th century two great modern dockyards were built, one at Wilhelmshaven on the North Sea and the other at Kiel on the Baltic; these were connected by a ship canal. Smaller establishments were maintained at Cuxhaven, Bremerhaven, Flensburg, Swinemünde, Danzig and Kiaochow in the Far East.

It was a time when political intrigue consumed Europe. Great nations entered into alliances to preserve the balance of power, and the small nations, jealous of their sovereignty and fearful of being swallowed by their greedy neighbours, plotted with and against each other. Serbia resented having two-thirds of her blood-brothers oppressed by Austria–Hungary where they lived. The quarrels of these two states involved the great powers. Russia and France supported Serbia; Germany, fearing both, supported Austria–Hungary. England, apprehensive of Germany's naval programme, leaned towards Russia and France. Europe was divided into hostile camps and fear dominated all politics, thus creating fresh problems and difficulties. Serbia was incensed because the great powers ignored her grievance and were scarcely sensible that her dream of unity existed, though this was the chief threat to European peace. A crisis in 1908 was averted, but relations between England and Germany deteriorated, and when Sir Charles Hardinge warned the Kaiser of the dangers of naval competition, the Kaiser answered that he would rather fight than submit to the dictation of his naval programme by a foreign power.

In the autumn of 1908 the British Admiralty learned that the German naval programme of 1909–10 was already being acted upon. In fact, in that year Admiral von Tirpitz laid down four 'all-big-gun' ships to Britain's two, and in 1909 he laid down four more. When, in the spring of 1909, this was revealed in the House of Commons, agitation began for an increase in the Government naval building programme and for eight *Dreadnought*s to be laid down; a popular slogan of the times was: 'We want eight and we won't wait'.

A compromise was reached whereby four ships were laid down at once and four more were to be laid down 'upon need being shown'. But public opinion caused the whole eight to be laid down at once, and between 1909 and 1911 England had built 18 *Dreadnought*s against Germany's nine.

In 1909 Bethmann-Hollweg was appointed Chancellor of Germany. Although sincere and earnest, he had no influence with the Kaiser or the heads of various ministries, and this included von Tirpitz at the Admiralty. In his memoirs he says he could do little for peace. Actually he could do little to reduce the naval programme either, for Tirpitz had the public and the press behind him and they were not at all disturbed that the rate at which the building of the fleet continued was arousing increased antagonism against Germany. By 1910, for example, her steam-fleet was three times as great as that of France.

One crisis followed another over the acquisition of territory in Africa by the European powers. Then Italy annexed territory from Turkey who had done her no harm, while the outbreak of the Balkan War in 1912 compelled Turkey to accept the position. Russia and England were also at loggerheads over Russia's attempts to annex Tehran from Persia. Then Winston Churchill offended Germany in a speech which described German's fleet as a luxury, but England's as a necessity; a few months later he aggravated the situation when he informed the House of Commons that Germany's new programme involved not only an increase in ships and personnel but also an increase in the fighting efficiency of her peacetime forces. A Franco–British naval convention was signed in September 1912, and this sealed British estrangement from Germany. England now concentrated her fleet in the North Sea, and France hers in the Mediterranean.

The Balkan War ran into 1913. To the amazement of the great powers, Turkey's German-trained army was thrashed; despised Serbia emerged as a triumphant victor and her allies, Greece and Rumania, joined with her in the expectation of uniting all their kinsmen in the Balkans and extending their territories. The balance of power was upset. The great powers were drawn into the Balkan struggles where the victors were already dissatisfied with their gains. The Bulgars secretly attacked the

Serbs and refused to surrender Salonika to Greece. Another war left Bulgaria helpless. Turkey and Rumania had contributed to her downfall and the decisions of the great powers were ignored by all the contestants, none of whom really expected that any treaties made in 1913 would be permanent. Russia and France came near to war with Germany over her penetration into Turkey's military machine but decided against it in view of England's possible reactions.

In Serbia, student agitation was bubbling over. Some of their demonstrations had ended in bloodshed and, in March 1914, the attempted assassination of an Austrian Archduke was narrowly prevented. Inside Austria–Hungary, anti-government agitation was even worse than in Serbia. It needed only a spark to explode the powder-barrel and there was not long to wait. 'The lamps are going out all over Europe,' said Sir Edward Grey, Foreign Secretary, 'we shall not see them lit again in our lifetime.'

At the end of June, Franz Ferdinand, Archduke of Austria, took his wife Sophie to Sarajevo in Bosnia where she was to make her first appearance in state. No special security arrangements had been made for the four cars which drove swiftly through the suburbs to the City Hall. A crack like a rifle shot was heard and a bomb exploded. A colonel was wounded and taken to hospital; the Archduke was uninjured. The bomb-thrower, an Austrian Serb, was caught. No military guard had been arranged to protect the Archduke who now altered the arranged programme and, accompanied by his wife, set off with the same cars to visit the wounded colonel.

By mistake the first car took the wrong turning; the others followed, then all the cars slowed down. Two shots were fired at less than ten feet. The Duchess sank unconscious upon her husband's breast. Blood was gushing from his mouth. The cars were driven to the Government building where doctors found a bullet in the Duchess' stomach and the Archduke dying from a severed artery in the neck. Both victims were given absolution by a Franciscan monk. Fifteen minutes later they were dead. The murderer, a Serbian high school student named Gabriel Princip, was seized by the crowd. He swallowed cyanide but vomited it up again.

The Kaiser received the news on the Imperial yacht *Hohenzollern* in Kiel Bay. He wore an admiral's uniform, for the first English ships to visit Kiel for 19 years were there.

The Austro–Hungarian Government accused the Serbian Government of complicity in the plot, although their own investigator had reported that it was 'definitely improbable'. Germany knew that to support Austria–Hungary would lead to war with Serbia, and in turn that would mean war with Russia also. On 26 July England's fleet, which had completed manoeuvres, did not disperse and was thus mobilised. On 29 July Russia executed a general mobilisation. Austria–Hungary followed suit the following day. On 31 July Germany heard of Russia's mobilisation, and on 1 August declared war upon her. France immediately declared general mobilisation and prepared to defend her frontier. Germany sent an ultimatum demanding to know if France would remain neutral in a Russo–German war. On the same day Belgium mobilised. Sir Edward Grey, who for some days had been living with Lord Haldane, Minister of War, received a despatch after dinner that an ultimatum had been delivered in Brussels demanding the free movement of German troops through Belgian territory. The two men walked across to the Prime Minister, Mr Asquith, and obtained his agreement to order immediate mobilisation of the army. Thanks to Churchill, the Navy was already prepared for war. Throughout Sunday 2 August, the Germans were marching towards the Belgian frontier, and by 18.30 hrs it was certain that they were about to cross it. Making a final bid to keep England neutral, Germany offered to preserve France's integrity, though not that of her colonies. She also hinted that Belgium's neutrality might be violated. This offer Grey stiffly refused. Churchill and Kitchener had always maintained that Germany meant to invade, and on 2 August their prophecies were fulfilled. A telegram from King Albert of Belgium appealing for help reached London.

On 3 August Germany declared war on France. At 09.30 hrs on 4 August, Grey demanded an immediate reply from Germany as to their intentions towards Belgium's neutrality. At 14.00 hrs, upon hearing that it had been violated, he instructed the British Ambassador in Berlin to demand 'a satisfactory reply' and to ask for his passports if he did not receive one by midnight. Upon the German Chancellor stating 'we must advance into France by the quickest and easiest route', relations were broken off, and at midnight England was at war. By the time peace returned, nine million people had died.

The British Navy faced the war with confidence. Despite Germany's utmost efforts in building a dozen ships of the *Dreadnought* class and eight large battlecruisers, the British fleet outranked Germany's by a ratio of three to two.

2

The Battle of Jutland

O N 31 MAY 1916 the German High Seas Fleet, under Vice-Admiral Reinhard Scheer, clashed with the British Grand Fleet under Admiral Sir J.R. Jellicoe in the battle of Jutland, called by the Germans the battle of Skagerrak. The main action took place about 75 miles from the German coast in latitude 57°N and longitude 6°E.

The British fleet was based at Scapa Flow, an area of sea in the south of the Orkneys bounded by the island of Pomona, or Mainland, on the north, by the islands of Burray and South Ronaldsay on the east, and by the islands of Flotta and Hoy on the south-west and west. Scapa Flow contains several small islands, and other islands lie in the channels leading into it. From north to south it measures some 15 miles and its average breadth is about eight miles. Its waters are sheltered, and its good anchorage had led to its selection by Admiral Jellicoe as the main naval base of the British fleet in preference to Cromarty Firth, though everything had to be improvised and guns landed from ships to strengthen the defences. One great disadvantage was the lack of a fully equipped dockyard nearer than those in the south of England. The Admiralty therefore despatched a floating dock to Invergordon in the Cromarty Firth, and work was accelerated on a new dockyard at Rosyth on the Firth of Forth. The yard was later used for breaking up salvaged German ships.

The British fleet consisted of the Admiral's flagship and attached ships, two battle squadrons of the British Grand Fleet, three cruiser squadrons, two complete flotillas and part of a third.

Vice-Admiral Scheer in his flagship *Friedrich der Grosse* commanded the Third Battle Squadron consisting of *König, Grosser Kurfürst, Kronprinz, Markgraf, Kaiser, Kaiserin* and *Prinzregent Luitpold*, scouting forces which included *Seydlitz, Moltke, Derfflinger* and *von der Tann*, together with several cruisers. The ships named above were among those later to be surrendered under the terms of the Armistice. The Fourth Scouting Group was commanded by Commodore Ludwig von Reuter, later Vice-Admiral.

The British Grand Fleet was supreme at sea, and the British naval command had no intention of gambling with it in night actions or where it might be at a disadvantage. British policy was to bring the enemy to action only when there was a fair degree of certainty that it could be destroyed.

The only important clash before the Battle of Jutland had been off the Dogger Bank fishing grounds in the North Sea where, on 24 January 1915, the Germans had intended to scatter the east-coast trawlers which, they believed, performed reconnaissance work for the Admiralty. The German intentions were known, as the Admiralty had a salvaged copy of the German navy's code-book. Beatty left Rosyth with a strong force, made a chance contact with the enemy, chased them across the North Sea but narrowly failed to bring them to battle. However, *Lion*, Beatty's flagship, set alight with her 13.5-inch guns two gun-turrets of Hipper's flagship, *Seydlitz*. This caused cordite fires, but three members of *Seydlitz*'s crew averted an explosion and saved their ship by managing to flood the magazines. *Moltke* was also hit, but British gunfire and communications were poor and advantage was not taken of it. Then *Derfflinger*'s 12-inch guns scored a hit on *Lion*. Beatty had to transfer his flag to a destroyer, and during this time his second-in-command, misled by the reading of a signal, let all the enemy ships escape except for *Blücher* which was sunk.

Thereafter the German High Seas Fleet had been kept ineffective by the British blockade, its crews chafing under inactivity. The policy of the German High Command was to avoid decisive action until the British fleet had been so weakened as to make a successful attack upon it probable. To this end German cruisers were to have bombarded Sunderland to tempt British cruisers into pursuing them into a pack of U-boats lurking off England's east coast. But as the weather was too bad for aerial reconnaissance, Scheer delayed his operations, unwilling to risk an approach to the English coast without full knowledge of his enemy's movements. However, his submarines could not lie in wait indefinitely, so Scheer changed his plans and on 30 May 1916 ordered a scouting force to demonstrate off the coast of Norway. This, he hoped, would draw out the British fleet and, by keeping out of sight behind his scouting force, he might fall upon and destroy a detached part of the enemy.

Jellicoe had been warned of impending German movements, and the battlecruiser fleet was ordered to proceed from Scapa Flow to a specified point off the Scottish coast. A similar order was sent to the sections of the Grand Fleet based at Invergordon and Rosyth. The few German submarine attacks were ineffective and failed to halt the fleet's progress.

On 31 May Jellicoe received a misleading telegram from the Admiralty that the German fleet was still in the Jade River in Heligoland Bay. To economise on fuel and believing that he had plenty of time in hand, he slowed down his destroyers. But the German fleet had sailed in the early hours of that morning, and its battle fleet was 50 miles astern of its scouting force. The German Commander-in-Chief, too, was misled by the wireless reports from his U-boats. Now, quite by chance, the British light cruiser *Galatea* and the German light cruiser *Elbing* simultaneously sighted a stray merchant steamer, the *N.J. Fjord*. Proceeding to investigate it, they sighted each other, and their signals to their respective flagships brought together sections of the opposing forces. The two cruisers had exchanged shots. *Elbing* was the first to claim a hit, though the shell failed to explode.

Unaware of greater German forces further south, Beatty, with his six battlecruisers *Indefatigable*, *Lion*, *Princess Royal*, *Queen Mary*, *Tiger* and *New Zealand*, began a brisk running fight with five German battlecruisers: *Lutzow*, *Derfflinger*, *Moltke*, *Seydlitz* and *von der Tann*. The British Fifth Battle Squadron was unfortunately five miles in the opposite direction to that in which the enemy had been sighted, and an imprecise signal from the cruisers' flagship led to further delay in bringing this force into action. As a result, the British battlecruisers suffered heavily. On the only occasion during the operations when a British aircraft was used for reconnaissance, its report was not received by the battlecruisers' flagship, while the flagship's signals for the distribution of fire were also interpreted incorrectly. After three minutes the Germans had scored eight hits on *Lion*, *Tiger* and *Princess Royal*. The first British hit was on *Seydlitz*, whose ammunition caught fire, and the ship was saved only by having her magazines flooded. Another misunderstanding had saved *Derfflinger* from being fired upon, but now she was engaged by *Queen Mary* who was soon scoring hits upon her. *Von der Tann* sank *Indefatigable* in a furious duel after three shells had exploded in her magazines, and 57 officers and 958 men of *Indefatigable's* complement were lost, the only two of her men saved being picked up by a German destroyer.

About 15 minutes after the action had opened, the British Fifth Battle Squadron managed to get within range of the enemy and opened fire on *von der Tann* at 19,000 yards. A 15-inch shell crashed into *von der Tann* on the water-line and 600 tons of water poured into her, but she was able to continue fighting. The German vessels in the rear were saved from destruction by the poor quality of British shells which burst without penetrating the enemy's armour.

After a brief pause the engagement was renewed and *Queen Mary* was attacked by *Derfflinger* and *Seydlitz*. An explosion caused by a salvo ripped her apart and she sank immediately with 57 officers and 1,209 men. Only eight of her crew were saved.

'There seems to be something wrong with our damned ships,' Beatty remarked. The main fault was the inadequate protection against the spread of fire from the gun-turrets.

At about this time two opposing destroyer flotillas came to grips between the lines of battlecruisers. The German flotillas fled towards the van of their battlecruisers pursued by two British destroyers, one of which was crippled by enemy fire. Another British destroyer was also left helpless between the lines.

The German battlecruisers were being sorely pressed when suddenly they sighted their battle fleet. Ten minutes previously Jellicoe had received a message that the High Seas Battle Fleet was coming north.

The German Commander-in-Chief believed that, after all, he had fallen upon a detached part of the British fleet, and he was so preoccupied with this that he missed the easy targets presented by the battlecruisers, each in turn, as they wheeled round the same point on their new course.

Beatty promptly re-engaged the enemy. Soon *Seydlitz* was holed again under water by a torpedo, but she was stoutly built and kept her place in the line. Hits were also registered on *Grosser Kurfürst* and *Markgraf.*

Scheer, in his flagship *Friedrich der Grosse,* was still unaware that the Grand Fleet was at sea but thought that, as he had planned, a part of it was in his grasp. In the van, as he sailed north-west in pursuit, were the seven battleships: *König, Grosser Kurfürst, Kronprinz, Markgraf, Kaiser, Kaiserin* and *Prinzregent Luitpold.* They were screened by four destroyer flotillas. Hipper did not share his superior's views, but his signalling was ineffective, so he had to resign himself to following the battleships, though he was still under heavy fire and his ships were badly mauled. *Derfflinger* in particular had suffered, while *Seydlitz* was down by the bows, kept afloat only by her watertight compartments.

Another of Beatty's signals was not seen in the Fifth Battle Squadron with the result that the two squadrons passed each other at high speed, one of them coming under the guns of the German battle fleet and receiving severe punishment. Firing became desultory as the British squadron drew out of range, and Beatty concentrated upon joining his Commander-in-Chief who was approaching from the north-west at the head of six lines of battleships headed by a cruiser squadron, his destroyer flotillas acting as a submarine screen.

The two battle fleets rushed towards each other at 40 knots, and at 14,000 yards the British battlecruiser fleet opened fire. Scarcely had Admiral Hipper turned away when the Third Battlecruiser Squadron engaged his Second Scouting Group. Ships on both sides were badly punished. Beatty lost touch with the enemy for some minutes but was then able to report its position, and Jellicoe deployed his ships in a formation which gave them an overwhelming tactical advantage, for they enveloped the head of the enemy's line in a way which let them give each other maximum support.

Meanwhile the First Cruiser Squadron had been scouting ahead of the battle fleet and was engaged with German cruisers. As it now came between the opposing battle fleets, two British ships were sunk. The smoke began to roll away disclosing to Scheer Jellicoe's trap, into which he was sailing. The signal had actually been hoisted for the Grand Fleet to close when Jellicoe had to cancel it because his line was not yet in position and the battlecruisers were not clear of his van. This forced him to deploy again and, to add to his misfortunes, *Invincible*, with over 1,000 officers and men, was torn apart by *Derfflinger* and *König*. Only five men were saved. *Wiesbaden* was disabled at the same time by British cruisers. *Warrior* and *Defence*, two armoured cruisers, came under heavy fire from *Derfflinger* and four other battleships when they approached to sink her. *Defence* blew up and *Warrior* was lucky to escape when the enemy's fire was turned from her to *Warspite* whose steering gear was damaged by a shell from *Kaiserin*.

But Scheer was still in danger. To escape, his destroyers put up a smoke-screen. Under its cover the German fleet disappeared after sinking their crippled light cruiser *Wiesbaden*. It was now 18.40 hrs with only two hours of daylight left. Jellicoe worked his way between the German fleet and the coast. Reports of enemy submarines influenced him to change course, and scarcely had he re-formed his divisions when the German ships reappeared out of the mist. Scheer later claimed that this move was intentional, but it is probable that it was the result of a mistake.

The battle fleets again re-engaged. The leading German ships were headed by *König* which received a hail of shell, and *Markgraf* was hit in the engine-room. The German fleet faced annihilation as the British ships took up their appointed positions. Hipper prepared to sacrifice his cruisers to save his battle fleet, and they were hurled forward in a mass attack, later termed by the Germans 'a death ride'. Upon receiving the signal, 'Charge the enemy; ram, ships are to attack regardless of consequences', *Derfflinger* led *Seydlitz, Moltke* and *von der Tann* upon the enemy. *Derfflinger* had two turrets shattered and was hit repeatedly. All in *von der Tann's* control turret were killed by a direct hit, and only one gun still fired. The other two were also badly damaged and received permission to withdraw. One German destroyer was sunk and several others badly damaged in this gallant action to cover the withdrawal. Their torpedoes were fired from a range of 7,000 yards and they then laid a smoke-screen. Six of their destroyers were put out of action, and another was sunk by a direct hit. The 28 torpedoes they fired all missed their targets, but they forced Jellicoe to turn his battleships and take avoiding action, and by doing so he increased his distance from the enemy and so missed the chance of a decisive victory.

The three German battleships damaged were *Markgraf, Grosser Kurfürst* and *König*, but all their guns were serviceable and they were able to keep their place in the line. *Grosser Kurfürst* had shipped 800 tons of water and *König* 1,600 tons.

Beatty's signal to Jellicoe, which if acted upon promptly could have enabled him to cut off the whole of the enemy's battle fleet, caused such loss of time in its ciphering, transmission and deciphering, that contact with the enemy was temporarily lost again.

When Beatty next sighted the German battlecruisers and some battleships sailing south, he opened fire and was inflicting heavy punishment on the battered enemy battlecruisers, when they decided that they had suffered enough and sought cover behind their Second Battle Squadron. *Derfflinger's* remaining turret was put out of action, and *Seydlitz* hit yet again, while three old battleships which had gone to their aid were also damaged. Once again Jellicoe knew nothing of the affair, and this time *Lion's* wireless was also inoperable. Jellicoe was about to renew his engagement when Scheer realised his danger, turned hastily, and by 20.35 hrs had disappeared for the second time. Firing then died away and darkness fell.

At 21.00 hrs Jellicoe ordered his fleet to take up night cruising stations, hoping to deny the enemy their own coast and to finish the fight on the following day. Scheer made his night preparations also, but the battered Lützow was steadily sinking, and finally had to be abandoned and sunk. Both fleets groped their way into the darkness. Shortly after 22.00 hrs the German light cruisers ran into the right wing of the British flotillas bringing up the rear of the Grand Fleet. The British won a slight advantage in the sharp engagement that followed, and now other sections of the two fleets came into conflict. *Southampton* was soon ablaze from stem to stern, yet even in this condition she sank *Frauenlob* with a torpedo. After a quarter of an hour of furious fighting, the Germans withdrew.

Throughout the night there were encounters, as British destroyers threw themselves desperately in the path of an enemy who was as desperately trying to reach home. Two German destroyers rammed each other in the confusion; another was torpedoed and had to be sunk. British destroyers also suffered badly. Scheer was determined to break through at all costs and escape before daybreak. Then two British ships rammed each other and one had to be sunk. *Fortune, Ardent* and *Turbulent* were lost, and the armoured cruiser *Black Prince*, which strayed into the German battle fleet, was sunk at point-blank range.

Steadily the German fleet approached safety, and throughout the night only inaccurate information of its movements reached Jellicoe. Before daybreak the German ships had passed through the British light forces and were steaming eastward.

At about 13.45 hrs the Twelfth Flotilla sighted large ships steering south-east and they sank the battleship *Pommern*, but neither the British commander's wireless messages nor his report reached Jellicoe.

At about 14.25 hrs four destroyers sighted the enemy. They sank the German destroyer *V4*, but did not report it. That virtually ended the battle, for Scheer ordered his whole fleet to return to harbour. *Seydlitz*, with 5,000 tons of water in her hold, ran aground near the Horns Reef lightship, but a salvage vessel from Wilhelmshaven got her away by mid-morning.

On the British side bad communications, and on the German side poor tactics, contributed to a result which at the time seemed indecisive, though the British Grand Fleet was left in possession of the seas.

British losses were: three battlecruisers, three cruisers and eight destroyers, and 6,274 officers and men killed or taken prisoner. German losses were: one battleship, one battlecruiser, four light cruisers and eight destroyers; 2,545 officers and men were killed; there were no prisoners. British ships amounting to 115,025 tons had been destroyed compared with German losses of 61,180 tons.

Apart from cruiser squadrons and destroyers the British had 28 battleships and eight battlecruisers against Germany's 22 battleships and five battlecruisers.

On paper the advantage lay with the Germans who claimed the battle as a victory. But the German fleet ventured only once more out of harbour. That was on 19 August of the same year, but when Scheer was told that the British fleet was advancing to meet him, he returned to his base. In November 1918, when ordered to break the blockade, the crews mutinied and refused to weigh anchor. 'Why go out and die,' they asked, 'when peace is at hand?' Stokers drew the fires and refused to sail. At last Admiral von Hipper ordered the fleet to disperse to its harbours, and mutiny spread from ship to ship. By 7 November only the submarines were not flying the Red Flag. Kiel and Wilhelmshaven fell under the rule of a Soviet of Workers, Soldiers and Sailors, its president being an ex-stoker supported by a council of 21 with an inner council of five. When the war was lost to Germany, the fleet was in the hands of communist sailors who had to be persuaded to accept the authority of officers during the last inglorious voyage which the ships were to make under German crews.

Under the terms of the armistice, Germany agreed to surrender to Great Britain: ten battleships, six battlecruisers, eight light cruisers, 50 destroyers and all her submarines. These were her newest ships. A few others were added to the French and Italian navies, and she was allowed to keep some of her old vessels.

Of the surrendered capital ships, the number of hits received by them at Jutland were as follows:

Kaiser	2	*Derfflinger*	20
König	10	*Seydlitz*	24
Grosser Kurfürst	8	*Moltke*	4
Markgraf	5	*von der Tann*	4

3

Surrender

ON 15 NOVEMBER 1918 Rear-Admiral Sinclair sailed out with a light cruiser squadron to meet *Königsberg*, which was bringing Rear-Admiral Meurer and four of his staff officers to discuss the procedure for the surrender of the German fleet at a conference aboard *Queen Elizabeth*. *Königsberg* was brought to anchorage in a white fog, her guns screened under canvas covers. An outlandish row of men in black hats on her deck were members of the Workmen's and Soldiers' Council who had decided to accompany the Rear-Admiral, though Admiral Sir David Beatty had flatly refused to meet their delegates. No guard of honour met the admiral when he stepped aboard, and arms were not presented.

At 22.00 hrs the proceedings ended and the German officers left, watched by a dark, silent crowd of bluejackets. Meurer was a man of medium build. The blue cloak which fell to his heels rested on the end of his scabbard. Beneath his gold-peaked cap, his face with its short, trimmed grey beard looked small. The quartermaster shrilled his pipe. Meurer slightly inclined his head, then his chin fell to his breast as he passed down the side and into the darkness of the night.

There was a story current in the fleet that a marine on duty peeping through a keyhole 'saw one of the Huns seize something off the table and cram it into the pocket of his greatcoat, and a subsequent search of the greatcoat revealed a large lump of cheese'.

On 16 November Chancellor Ebert of Germany communicated to all U-boat crews and shipyard labourers the contents of a letter he had received from the German Armistice Commission. It said that the Commission had received an assurance from Admiral Rosslyn Wemyss that crews of the submarines handed over to the British would be released immediately after the delivery of the boats at ports indicated by the British Admiralty. Failure to deliver them would result in the cancellation of the armistice, and crews were warned not to burden themselves with a crime which would cause a renewal of bloodshed. Each married man who helped to deliver a vessel would receive 500 marks, and each single man 300 marks. The lives of all men would be insured by the German government.

Early in the morning of 20 November Rear-Admiral Sir Reginald Tyrwhitt, flying his flag in the light cruiser *Curaçao* with the light cruisers *Danae, Coventry, Centaur* and *Dragon* in his wake, waited at a point 35 miles from the Essex coast to receive the surrender of the German submarines. To port and starboard escorting destroyers formed dim shapes in the darkness. By 06.30 hrs the stars were beginning to fade and 20 minutes later, as a rosy glow overspread the thin mist, visibility improved and 'action stations' was sounded. A few minutes after 07.00 hours, in the cold light of dawn, five British light cruisers escorted by destroyers and guarded by minesweepers received the surrender of 20 German submarines.

The sun had barely risen when a British rigid airship of the Zeppelin type, the *R26* from Harwich, sailed down the line at 800 feet followed by a silvery Blimp and three flying-boats. *Dragon*, a new, spick-and-span ship, led the course back, the U-boats dark, humped lines on the sea. Behind *Dragon* sailed the transports, then a destroyer with five U-boats in her wake, then more destroyers and more U-boats. Two hours elapsed before the last vessel passed the flagship.

Off Harwich, the U-boats stopped their engines. Men stepped from their conning towers and stood silently on deck. Motor launches alongside the destroyers embarked the British crews who were to take over. The surrender was concluded in silence. There were no cheers, and there was no fraternising. The numbers on the U-boats had been painted out, and only one,

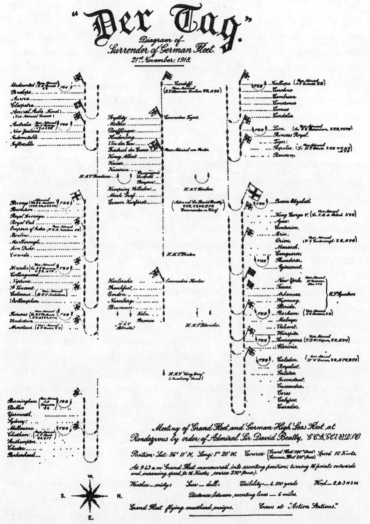

Plan of the surrender of the German fleet on 21 November 1918. A copy of this diagram was presented to all senior officers and officials present. (Courtesy of S.A. Brooks and H. Burd.)

U-107, flew the German Ensign. The White Ensign was promptly run up over it. Each British officer saluted as he stepped aboard. No other courtesy was paid. The German captains produced their papers; the British officers taking over produced their authorising papers; the German crews were sent forward. A German officer wept; another protested against having to carry on duty after surrender. The U-boats were taken by groups of five into Harwich harbour, the Germans standing on deck. No untoward incident had occurred other than the loss of one U-boat which had sunk on the voyage across the North Sea. Each submarine was in running order with periscope intact and torpedoes unloaded, as required by the terms of the armistice. By Saturday of the same week 96 U-boats had surrendered and their crews had returned to Germany. By 20 November 129 submarines had been escorted into harbour. Eye-witnesses said that the officers looked glum, but that the men were bright and cheerful.

The German High Seas Fleet surrendered on 21 November. A few minutes before 04.00 hrs the British First Battle Squadron led by *Revenge*, the flagship of Vice-Admiral Madden, began to move from the Firth of Forth towards their beaten enemies. Fog, which had been heavy, lifted, but clouds obscured the moon and stars. Ship followed ship. By daybreak the Grand Fleet, under Admiral Beatty in *Queen Elizabeth*, had taken up position in the open sea in two columns in single line ahead. Treachery was not expected, but all was ready to blow the German ships out of the water if any tricks were attempted.

Units of France, America and the dominions of Australia, Canada, South Africa and New Zealand were present with the British Navy.

At 08.30 hrs the German fleet was sighted by destroyers. An hour later the sun rose, and then there came into view a 'sausage' balloon towed by *Cardiff*, and through the murk behind there emerged the first of the German ships. At 09.40 hrs contact was made by the fleet.

Between the lines of waiting Allied vessels came the great fleet headed by the battleship *Friedrich der Grosse*. Then came the other eight battleships: *König Albert, Kaiser, Kronprinz Wilhelm, Kaiserin, Bayern* – which had never fired her guns in action,

Markgraf – one of the most powerful battleships in the German navy until the arrival of *Bayern* with her 15-inch guns, *Prinzregent Luitpold* and *Grosser Kurfürst*. Behind them at intervals of three cables sailed five battlecruisers of the *Kaiser* class: *Seydlitz* – bearing scars received at the battle of Dogger Bank in January 1915 and flying the broad pennant of Commodore Taegert, *Derfflinger* – also badly battered at Dogger Bank, *Hindenburg*, *Moltke* and *von der Tann* – which had suffered heavily in the British naval raid on Cuxhaven. Next came eight light cruisers headed by *Karlsruhe* flying the broad pennant of Commodore Harder. Finally, led by the British destroyer *Castor* flying the pennant of Commodore Tweedie, came 49 destroyers of the latest type from the 1st, 2nd, 3rd, 6th, 7th and 17th flotillas. One destroyer, *V30*, had been sunk by a mine on the passage from Germany with the loss of two men dead and three injured. At an order from Admiral Beatty, the allied ships turned 16 points so that the German ships were sandwiched.

The late Admiral W.E. Parry reflected the feeling of many officers and men when he wrote at the time in a private letter:

> It seems incredible from what we knew of the German Naval Officers that they would ever consent to surrender their ships. News filtered through, however, that there had been a meeting at all the naval ports, that the crews had seized the ships, killed various officers, hoisted the Red Flag, and demanded peace at once.

And a little later, when the surrendered fleet was inspected:

> The *strange dream* feeling persisted in remaining; it didn't seem possible that these were the ships we had been looking for for four years, that the rather indistinct grey form I had to keep peering at over the azimuth of the compass, was really the same as the silhouette labelled *Königsberg* class in my silhouette book.

Midshipman Keighley of *Repulse* commented that 'they won't go down to posterity with much honour and glory', and there were many, as tension grew, who could not believe that their enemy could surrender so tamely and said, 'Now they'll fire! They're bound to! They can never stand this.' But there was no untoward incident.

Headed by *Cardiff*, the German ships passed between the lines, looking like whales towed by a minnow. This time there were cheers as the escorting vessels passed the flagship. So great an expanse of sea was covered by the German fleet and the surrounding British warships that the head and rear of the columns were lost to sight in the haze. Slowly the ships moved towards their anchorage off May Island in the Firth of Forth, some miles to the east of the bridge.

About an hour before noon, Admiral Beatty signalled to the German ships, all of which were flying the German naval flag at their main, 'The German flag will be hauled down at sunset today, Thursday, and will not be hoisted again without permission.'

The inspection of the surrendered ships began on 22 November.

On Saturday 23 November, 20 of the surrendered destroyers escorted by 20 British destroyers steamed into the grey waters of the Flow through Hoxa Sound, between low-lying Flotta to port and Hoxa's lighthouse on the flat cape to starboard. Beyond Flotta rose Hoy's three hills. The bleak prospect could do nothing to raise the morale of the dispirited crews. The rest of the surrendered fleet arrived in batches: on Sunday 20 more destroyers escorted as before by 20 British destroyers; on Monday five battlecruisers and ten destroyers escorted by the First Battlecruiser Squadron; on Tuesday five battleships and four light cruisers escorted by five ships of the Second Light Cruiser Squadron; on Wednesday four battleships and three light cruisers escorted by four ships of the First Battlecruiser Squadron and four of the Third Light Cruiser Squadron.

On 3 December the first two transports, *Sierra Ventana* and *Graf Waldersee*, arrived at Scapa Flow to repatriate the surplus members of the German crews. A few days later four more transports arrived in pairs. On 4 December a German battleship, a light cruiser and a destroyer were sent to Scapa Flow to make up the deficiency of surrendered ships, and on 10 January 1919, as there was still one ship short, *Baden* was sent in place of the battlecruiser *Mackensen*, making in all 74 vessels interned there. The total care and maintenance party numbered 1,800 men.

On 13 December the last home-going transports left Scapa Flow. Von Reuter joined this last party, reckoning his time away as leave. He returned to Scapa Flow on 25 January 1919.

The condition of the ships and the lack of discipline struck all visitors. Midshipman Keighley commented: 'they were all rather dirty and crowds of men were watching us'. *Moltke's* captain was described as a good fellow, but brokenhearted and a complete wreck. The ship's magazines were full of potatoes and other objects. There was some 'porridgy stuff' in the galley, and upon being asked what it was, a German answered shortly, 'bloody birds' food'. Several German officers said they were glad to be there as they had feared they would probably be 'blotted out by the ship's crew on the way over'. On some ships all orders were taken from the Workmen's and Soldiers' delegates. Sometimes the men were respectful to the British, at other times effusive and sycophantic, but more often surly. *Moltke's* Workmen's and Soldiers' leader was a petty officer who was virtually senior to his captain. In one ship an inspecting officer was kept waiting for 40 minutes, and then, to all his questions merely received the off-hand reply, 'I really don't know' – an answer which was often given to search parties. Before the inspecting officer left, with quiet satisfaction he gave the same answer to the German captain who asked if he could say whether peace negotiations had started.

Admiral Parry found that *Karlsruhe* was 'filthy and couldn't have been cleaned for weeks'; eight of her 12 boilers were in such bad condition that they could not have stood much steaming. As for *Bayern*, she was completely controlled by six lower deck ratings.

Emden's ladder was down, but no officer was present to receive the search party. Captain Becker, still wearing the black Iron Cross with its silver edges, had been in command for only a few weeks, and he doubtless regretted even that short period, for the members of the Soviet in his ship answered their superiors without removing the cigarettes from their mouths and saluted British officers while ignoring their own. (There were, of course, two ships named *Emden*, the other being the notorious raider which was finally hunted down by the Australian light cruiser *Sydney* off the Cocos Islands.)

Discontent in *Friedrich der Grosse* erupted into drunkenness, rioting and violence in which the Red Guards participated, so much so that von Reuter had to request the return of mutineers and other bad characters. Some time about the middle of June the worst of the crews were returned to Germany, and by the 17th of the month, when the last steamer left for Germany with the final batch of repatriated men, 2,200 malcontents had been withdrawn from Scapa Flow. About this time Admiral von Reuter transferred to *Emden* with British permission because, it was said, he could no longer bear the appalling clatter of mutinous sailors roller-skating on the iron deck of *Friedrich der Grosse*.

4

Scuttled!

THE GERMAN FLEET'S ANCHORAGE in Scapa Flow was in the Bring Deeps, that part of the Flow lying roughly between the island of Hoy and the smaller islands of Graemsay and Fara. Von Reuter was depressed by his first sight of it:

> Nothing but mountainous, rocky islands, the naked rock showing through the heather – farm houses of local grey stone with barracks and hangars relieving the sameness, but the general impression one of ugliness.

The absence of trees adds to the low, bleak aspect of the islands and, because of particularly violent winds, trees can grow only in sheltered valleys. On some 24 days of the year winds of gale force usually blow from the Atlantic and, less frequently, but more violently, from the north-east. Tremendous rollers crash against cliffs and send spray hundreds of feet into the air. Ordinary gales occur at any time.

Cloudy skies and scanty sunshine must have aggravated the depression of the German crews, and even in still weather shipping is often endangered by dense white sea fogs.

Violence was in the air, and it was no stranger to the Orkneys. Vikings had used them as a convenient base for raids down the east and west coasts of Scotland, and in the last half of the ninth century King Harald Finehair of Norway had chased his enemies right across the North Sea, seized the Orkneys and established there a strong earldom. In September 1066 Harald Hardrada

25

had assembled a fleet there before sailing south to meet his fate fighting against the English King Harold at the battle of Stamford Bridge. Traces of Viking occupation are in the flat stones they used for their dry-stone walls, in a boat burial found by excavation, and in topographical names. It is possible that the blood of Black Danes runs in the veins of those broadheaded, dark people of the Orkneys today. In the early days of World War I there were several scares, all unfounded, that enemy submarines had penetrated Scapa Flow. In November 1914 a German submarine was destroyed in the outer approaches and, in 1918, after the mutiny in the German fleet, submarine *U18* was manned entirely by German officers in a last desperate attempt to avenge their dishonour; it was rammed off Mainland and rendered in a sinking condition by the armed trawler *Dorothy Gray*, the first auxiliary vessel to sink a submarine, before it sank it was rammed again by *Garry*, a destroyer which hurried to the scene in response to a signal from *Dorothy Gray*.

Now the lines of surrendered ships extended from the Barrel of Butter Buoy round by the north end of the small island of Cava, and then between Fara and Hoy. Some, but not all, of the enemy ships were within sight of the British ships. Technically the ships were interned and not surrendered, for the peace treaty was yet to be signed, and British crews could not therefore be placed aboard.

A German caretaker crew on a battleship and on a battlecruiser consisted of about 200 officers and men. Destroyers were lashed together in pairs and threes. Each 'bundle' had a company of from 12 to 20 men. All fittings of value, such as scientific instruments, had been removed from the ships before their departure from Germany, together with considerable quantities of their metal work. The Germans were not, of course, allowed either arms or ammunition. After internment at Scapa Flow, maintenance parties were not allowed ashore, and four drifters maintained a 24-hour patrol of the anchorage. Each drifter carried an armed party and a 12-pounder gun. The Germans had to organise their own food supply as no one else would supply them with provisions.

As time passed, indiscipline increased among the crews, and

many of the officers became despondent. 'I am detaining you', one British commander said to a German captain whose ship he had inspected, 'No doubt you have things to do.' 'There is nothing for me to do now but think,' was the reply, 'and my thoughts are not pleasant.' Life for the Germans was extremely boring. Men constantly reported sick, and many were mutinous.

The naval conditions of the peace terms had been signed in June 1918, but there was considerable wrangling among the Allies about the final disposal of the surrendered ships. Great Britain wanted to have them destroyed, but France and the other Allies, desirous of reducing Britain's marked superiority in naval strength, wished to have them shared out and added to their respective fleets. Von Reuter settled the matter for them.

As early as 1 June he had secretly made preparations for the fleet to be scuttled, 'a move which would take place,' he notified the German commanders under him, 'if the English try to take us by force, or if a special order comes from me', and he gave the code words he would use to signify that all torpedo tubes, valves and other apertures were to be opened, and left open in such a way that they could not readily be closed again, and that ships were then to be scuttled immediately.

On 20 June 1919 *Emden* had been seen to fly signals at her peak which had apparently been answered by the rest of the interned fleet.

The upper flag was a white ball on a blue pennant, the lower one a yellow and blue pennant. This seemingly aroused no suspicions that anything unusual was afoot, though later there were those who said that the British had deliberately ignored what was going on.

On the morning of 21 June the British First Battle Squadron and its escorting destroyers left Scapa Flow on an exercise. One British destroyer remained on duty in Scapa Flow. Two others were there undergoing repairs; there were also a few drifters and trawlers and one depot ship. Bernard F. Gribble, the marine artist, was aboard *Sochosin*, an Admiralty trawler, making official drawings of the German ships; he noticed that all vessels were still flying the two code flags. But neither he, nor the lieutenant commanding *Sochosin* whose attention he drew to the unusual happening, knew that when von Reuter was informed of the departure of the British First Battle Squadron, he had ordered the pre-arranged code signal to be hoisted: *Schiffe sofort versenken* (Sink all ships immediately). Even had they seen it and been able to translate it correctly it is doubtful if it would have aroused suspicion, for it merely read: *Paragraph 11. Bestätigen.* (Paragraph 11. Confirm.)

It needed little more effort to sink a ship than to pull a plug from a bath. All that was necessary was the turning of a valve wheel, a procedure occupying no more than a few seconds. Most of the other apertures, such as ventilators, scuttles, hatches and bulkheads were already open. But the Germans did more than merely leave them open. They did their best to ensure that they could not be closed again. They could drain every compartment of their battleships by means of two 24-inch pipes, one along each side of the double bottom. A valve enabled each compartment to be flooded or emptied, and this valve had a control rod which passed to the armoured deck and worked through a universal joint situated at the bottom. When the ships were scuttled, the universal joints were disconnected so that it became impossible to pump compartments dry separately. When salvage work finally began it was therefore impossible to stabilise a ship by isolating its various compartments.

At 11.45 hrs Mr Gribble saw German sailors aboard *Friedrich der Grosse* throwing baggage into boats. The same thing was happening on *Frankfurt*. Boats were being lowered, and men were scrambling into them. *Sochosin's* skipper headed for the nearest ship, which happened to be *Frankfurt*, and ordered his men to be ready with rifles and cutlasses. He shouted an order to the Germans in boats to return immediately to their ships.

'We have no oars,' shouted the sailors who had thrown them away. A British sailor immediately threw several into the sea for them. Two German officers in the boats were impudent and demanded to be taken aboard, but the boats which came alongside were kept off at gunpoint.

A drifter which had an equally early view of the scuttling was *Trust-on* which was transferring stores received from Germany to *Emden*. They were just casting off after finishing their work when a crowd of German ratings rushed from amidships begging to be taken off as the ship was sinking. *Emden* was already settling by the stern when von Reuter forced a way through the ratings and their officers. The officers wore Number One uniforms and were carrying suitcases and parcels. Von Reuter ordered the skipper of the drifter to take him and his crew aboard the British flagship, and received a curt refusal. *Trust-on* headed at full speed to *Victorious*, a workshop and dockyard ship which lay at the southern end of the Sound. When *Trust-on* reached her, Rear-Admiral Prendergast was reading a signal from the guardship *Westcott* that *Friedrich der Grosse* was sinking and that, contrary to orders, all German ships were wearing ensigns and battle-flags. He lost no time in despatching a signal to Vice-Admiral Fremantle of the First Battle Squadron who ordered the recall of the battleships and almost all the destroyers based on Scapa Flow. He then took a small party in his pinnace and managed to board one of the destroyers. But it was already sinking, so he took off the crew and put them under an armed guard in *Victorious* as prisoners-of-war.

Meanwhile other crews equipped with lifebelts took to their boats, while the more daring members leapt overboard. Before assistance could arrive, most of the ships were entirely under the water, and others had only their mastheads visible on which flew the white ensign. Tugs, drifters and trawlers co-operated in efforts to save the vessels still afloat. The local Admiralty Port Officers managed to beach 11 destroyers. The crew of the depot ship *Sandhurst* kept four afloat and beached seven more. *Baden* which had taken no part in the affair and two light cruisers were beached at Swanbister Bay, and one light cruiser was beached off Cava.

A party of children enjoying a pleasure trip in the steamer *Flying Kestrel* had something to talk about for the rest of their lives. As they steamed between the lines of ships on their way home they saw the ships beginning to sink. *Flying Kestrel* put ashore her passengers at Stromness, then returned to assist with the beaching operations.

Admiral Sir Henry McCall, then First Lieutenant in *Westcott*, the guard ship, left the following account of the scuttling:

At the time, *Westcott* was at immediate notice for steam at a buoy in Gutter Sound where there was a view of the greater part of the interned fleet. The Battle Squadron with its attendant cruisers and destroyers had gone into Pentland Firth for gunnery practice. *Westcott* was the only British ship in harbour apart from the depot ship and one destroyer which was boiler-cleaning alongside a couple of fleet trawlers. The officers were all gathered in the ward room having a gin before lunch when a sub-lieutenant officer of the watch on the quarter deck shouted through the ward room hatch, 'There's a German destroyer sinking.' Lieutenant-Commander Peploe, the skipper, answered, 'Don't talk such tripe.' But they all hurried on deck and saw that every German ship had hoisted its flag and that ladders were being got out and boats lowered. A signal was at once sent to the Vice-Admiral who was at sea.

Peploe decided to leave a bellicose petty officer behind in a skiff with orders to beach as many destroyers as possible by parting their cables, thus allowing them to drift ashore. About eight were dealt with before the rest settled. Peploe attempted to adopt the same procedure with *Hindenburg*, whose caretaker crew was pouring down the gangway into a couple of launches as *Westcott* drew alongside. The Germans ignored orders to go back, so Peploe spattered the sides of *Hindenburg* with a machine-gun just before the gangway as the last men tumbled into the boats. The Germans then threw up their hands shouting *Kamerad*, but their boats drifted away as there was no one to keep them to the gangway. Peploe ordered his whaler to be lowered and *Hindenburg* to be boarded so that her stopcocks could be closed.

Lunch could only have just begun in the ward room at the time of scuttling. In cabins outside there was every sign of belongings having been seized in haste, evidence that the order to scuttle had come as a surprise. All lights were out in the engine-room, and as this was probably caused by the ship sinking and letting in water, the boarders hurriedly regained the upper deck. One of them later told the reporter of the *Orcadian*, a Kirkwall newspaper:

> I went on board the *Hindenburg* when she was sinking to shut down all the doors we could find. It was awful on board, you could hear the swishing of the water in the boiler-rooms and see the oily surface of the water getting gradually higher and higher. We closed as many doors as we could, but it was no use and eventually she sank. One diesel engine was still running making the electric light, so we could

still see a bit, but it stopped suddenly when the water came upon it, and we were plunging into absolute darkness on board the sinking Hun. Luckily we had some hand lamps with us, so we could see a little. When we had closed as many doors as possible, we had to come away as there was great danger of one of the boilers bursting. The ship was also beginning to heel dangerously. We went back to get some dynamite to blast cables as we could not part them on board; we had to blow them up so that the ship could drift ashore. However, she sank before drifting ashore. The cabins and everything were in complete disorder where things had been snatched up hurriedly. I bashed in a portrait of old Hindenburg with a hammer. In the Ward Room were silver cups etc, but we could not take anything as there was too much hurry.

At the coxswain's suggestion, the cable was parted after TNT had been lashed to it above the waterline. As she was sinking more slowly than most of the ships, British tugs took her in tow intending to beach her on Cava Island, but just off shore she began to settle in shallow water on an even keel with her upper decks just awash and her funnels, masts and upper gun turret showing above water. Destroyers and tugs tried to move her, but suddenly she rolled over and had to be abandoned.

It was now too late to attend to the other ships, for two hours after the first alarm the whole of the German fleet was sinking in various stages. Boats and rafts and men in life-jackets were everywhere. Some men had not put on their jackets properly and when overcome by cold floated head down with their feet sticking in the air.

After sinking the boats in which the crew were leaving their ship, *Westcott's* men boarded the sinking light cruiser *Nürnberg*, hauled down her ensign and slipped her cables so that she drifted ashore and beached herself. The drifter *Caersin* drove back deserting crews with rifle fire. The drifter *Clonsin* took the light cruiser *Dresden* in tow though her main deck was already awash. They were only a mile from Cava beach when *Dresden* sank so quickly that there was no time to cast off the tow rope. *Seydlitz* was boarded, but everything movable was wired fast and she had to be left to her fate.

The first destroyers of the First Battle Squadron returned at full speed at about 14.30 hrs when only two German battleships, one battlecruiser and four light cruisers remained afloat, and they were sinking. *Markgraf,* a battleship, was one of them, and her crew had not left when she was boarded by the crew of the drifter *Cabalsin;* they were obstructed by the Germans, and in the ensuing scuffle the captain of *Markgraf, a* married man with four children, was killed and her engineer officer seriously wounded. But nothing could be done to save *Markgraf,* and shortly after her captain's body had been taken off she went the way of the rest.

Von Reuter recorded in his book the various times at which the capital ships sank. The first was *Friedrich der Grosse* at 12.16 hrs followed by *König Albert* at 12.54 hrs. By 14.00 hrs 11 more had gone, by 15.00 hrs another four. *Karlsruhe* went down at 15.50 hrs, *Markgraf* at 16.45 hrs and last of all *Hindenburg* at 17.00 hrs. *Friedrich der Grosse* had gone down in a few minutes. *Brummer,* a cruiser of the *Emden* class, began to lean over and sink, her crew in boats cheering as she went under. From the number of lifebelts floating about, it was thought that many lives must have been lost. Despite the violence which had to be used against the Germans, only two officers and six men were killed and five wounded. Von Reuter said that four were killed and eight wounded, all of No VI Flotilla (German sources state that one officer and seven petty officers and men perished and 21 were wounded).

'Unconfirmed' and quite unveracious eye-witness accounts soon appeared in the local press. A member of a drifter's crew alleged that a German officer, who presumably had refused to sanction the action taken by his crew and was hated by them, had been strung up to the mast and had gone down with the ship. An extended version of the story alleged that several officers had been tied to the masts of their ships and had been drowned as the ships sank. On board a dirty destroyer a German officer 'dressed in a frock coat and black gloves' was seen standing on the deck of a sinking ship while the crew in small boats were stabbing each other. German officers were frequently seen to be using their revolvers against their men. Even more imaginative was the story of a girl who reported that her brother, employed in a vessel in the Flow, jumped into a boat and found himself in blood 'up to his knees', and that he saw a German surgeon lying dead with stab-wounds in his back.

On a hillside overlooking the scene, a young farm worker named A.S. Thomson had been approached excitedly by his brother who cried, 'Look! There's a sub.' 'That's no submarine,' answered the other, 'it's a German ship going down.' These two watched the whole dramatic event. Both were later to leave the farm and become divers with the salvage firm of Cox & Danks, with whom, at the time of writing, A.S. Thomson is still actively employed.

One of the *Trust-on* officers who later went aboard *Emden* said that von Reuter was flying his flag, a black cross like a Maltese Cross on a white ground, that the cabin was gaily decorated with flags and bunting and smelt strongly of tobacco and spirits as though a celebration party had been held the night before, and he also described her officers as wearing yellow kid gloves and smoking cigars – which sounds like another unveracious story.

Of all that great fleet which had so lately been the pride of the German people, only *Baden*, three cruisers and 18 destroyers remained afloat. The oil slicks of the sunken ships killed all life for years to come on the coasts where they settled. *Frankfurt* and *Emden* sank in shallow water in Swanbister Bay. Appendix 2 is a copy of a letter later recovered from *Emden's* safe in Admiral von Reuter's cabin. *Baden* was also beached there and later pumped dry and salvaged by the Admiralty.

The German crews were rounded up, and with von Reuter were placed in custody in British ships. British guards were placed in the ships which were saved. It was said that sounds like the firing of rifles were heard as some of the ships heeled over and sank.

This scuttling of the ships was a flagrant breach of the armistice terms, and von Reuter was angrily accused of treachery by Vice-Admiral Fremantle and made prisoner-of-war, while the crews were sent as prisoners to a military camp near Invergordon.

It was 14.30 hrs on 21 June when Fremantle paraded von Reuter and his officers and said, 'Before I send you ashore as a prisoner-of-war I would like to express to you my indignation at the deed which you have perpetrated, and which was that of a traitor violating the action of the arrangements entered into by the Allies. The German fleet was, in a sense, more interned than actually imprisoned. The vessels were resting here as a sort of goodwill from the German Government until Peace had been signed. It is not the first occasion on which the Germans have violated all the decent laws and rules of the sea.' Von Reuter, not unnaturally, considered that he had done only what Fremantle himself would have attempted had the positions been reversed.

On 24 June salvage advisers were sent by the Admiralty to survey the sunken ships and report on the possibility of raising them. The report concluded that little difficulty would be experienced in raising them by compressed air as they were undamaged. But the Admiralty had already decided that they were too heavy to be held by hawsers and that salvage was out of the question. An official statement was made on 23 June that the beached ships *Baden* and *Emden* would probably be salved, and possibly *Frankfurt* and *Nürnberg*, but as for the remainder, sunk in water from 12 to 20 fathoms deep and no danger to navigation, 'where they are sunk, they will rest and rust. There can be no question of salving them'.

However, in due course, the ships *were* a danger to navigation, and they *were* to be salved.

In October 1920 the Aberdeen trawler *Ben Urie, en route* for home, ran on to *Moltke* and remained fast for several hours. Reporting this incident, the *Orcadian* commented, 'Several trawlers have run on this battleship, and it is high time that greater precautions were taken to mark exactly where these sea monsters lie.' Another trawler ran on to the same wreck and was lying there helpless as darkness came. The distressed ship signalled with lights and blew loudly on her siren for assistance. A motor boat was sent from Cava, but meanwhile a drifter from Lyness had got her off. But luck was not with her, for almost immediately she went right on top of *Kaiser* only a few hundred yards away.

Relics from the scuttled ships were picked up almost daily for a considerable time on the Banffshire coast. A schoolboy found a wooden box full of postcards from a sailor's sweetheart. Another card requested payment for 2,000 cigarettes which the sailor denied having received. Boys played football with black bread baked at Kiel, mistaking them for dumplings, and

No. 3▲

No. 2▲ BAYERN

KAISER FRIEDRICH DER GROSSE GROSSER KURFÜRST CAVA No. 4▲

KÖLN (OR BRUMMER) BRUMMER (OR KÖLN)

KÖNIG ALBERT KRONPRINZ WILHELM

MARKGRAF

(Dries 6 ft.) KAISERIN KARLSRUHE

(Dries 9ft.)

LT. F. 40 FT. KÖNIG

No. 1▲ PRINZ REGENT LUITPOLD

DERFFLINGER KAISER (Dries 5ft.) DRESDEN

White House (conspicuous) CAVA

GREEN HEAD VON DER TANN HINDENBURG

MOLTKE (Dries 6 ft.) WARD POINT

SEYDLITZ 20 ft. high

V.86 (from F6) 2 Boats (G6) 6 in. 5 stort

G.89 (G9) Boat upright, Funnels showing

PEGAL HEAD

NORTH POINT

(J.1) B.110 (L1) B.98 (M4) G.56

RISA 2 Boats (K1) 2 Boats 0.50 right Aix Buoy

RISA SOUND 2 Boats, (N4) B.109 6.50 & V.83 Broken mast (P.1) B.124 H.169

2 Boats (Q.1) B.115 H.145 V.T.S (from F5) Boat badly broken up

E. Line Beacon G.101 & G.104 Mast down, 6 ft. below surface at L.W.

RISA BAY (R4) 2 Boats 6 M B.112 H.120

(S4) 2 boats (from (T4) B.111 H.95 B.110

HOY 2.35 & 6.25 ft.

Risa Lodge F (U4) V.70

MILL. BAY Mast down S LL. Buoy

Thompson's Hill

Work Shops LYNESS Pier FARA

Oil Tanks

WEDDEL SOUND

ORE BAY 2 Boats (O4) S.49 & S.50

4 M (P3) V.45 (Q.1)

FLOTTA

Map of Scapa Flow showing position of the sunk German fleet.

quantities of tea and soap were also washed up after having drifted 80 miles.

With the coming of peace, scrap-metal in enormous quantities was needed for post-war industries, and prodigious quantities of war material were available, so, for a year or two after the scuttling, the German ships lay undisturbed except for predatory raids upon them by Orcadian fishermen. It was not until world stocks of scrap showed signs of becoming exhausted that a wider interest was shown in the German ships.

5

The Men, the Means and the Ships

IN 1922 THE STROMNESS Salvage Syndicate bought a destroyer which was towed into harbour at Stromness for breaking up. This was the first ship of the German fleet to be taken away, and it ended up serving many useful domestic purposes. For example, its boiler tubes were polished and cut up and sold in thousands for curtain rods.

Then, on 26 April 1923, it was announced that 'the Admiralty have invited an eminent engineer and salvage expert to make an offer for the contract of raising the ships. If the scheme materialises it will be the means of absorbing considerable local labour for a year or two.' This promised to be a godsend to the islanders, for the Orkneys had been afflicted by terrible weather and poor crops, and fishing had been a failure.

In June 1923 it was stated that the Admiralty had sold a portion of the sunken fleet to a company headed by Mr J.W. Robertson, convenor of the county of Zetland, who was to direct salvage operations. Confirmation came from London that four torpedoboat destroyers were to be salved; these were near the island of Fara and in much shallower water than the capital ships. Robertson said he did not expect to begin operations until the following month, that he proposed to seal the ships hermetically, and when he had pumped them out sufficiently to contain flotation, salvage should not be difficult. During the summer months a certain amount of material was brought ashore, but nothing of great interest. However, Robertson was not idle and his company, the Scapa Flow Salvage & Shipbreaking Co Ltd, planned to lift the ships by methods entirely different from others subsequently employed.

Robertson acquired from the Admiralty two concrete barges, each approximately of 1,000 tons capacity. Between them they had a lifting capacity of 3,000 tons. Each barge had a length of 92 feet and a beam of 32 feet. They were to be moored 30 feet apart and spanned by eight lengths of steel girders, each weighing up to 24 tons. The outer edges of the decks on the barges were made level with concrete, to provide a flat bearing surface for the hard wood blocks and girders which were to be laid across the full beam of both barges. There were two tiers in each group of girders, and each tier was three tiers high, the lower line consisting of 17-inch by 6-inch H girders, the central line of 16-inch by 6-inch, and the top line of 12-inch by 6-inch ones. These were all held in place by steel plates and diaphragms needing in all some 20,000 bolts and nuts. Pulleys were then attached to the girders, two on each side, over which chains were to be passed and shackled to 16 steel belts under the destroyer.

This work was carried out, and the belts were held in position by distance pieces. When the chains came over the pulleys they were gripped by huge 7-foot eye-bolts with a heavy thread or worm. This passed through an eye with a large nut on the end. By turning the nuts with spanners – the large spanner was six feet long – the load was taken by the wires, and lifting began.

Robertson also proposed to assist lift and manoeuvrability by placing a large balloon (a 'camel' or air bag), capable of lifting over 100 tons, directly above the destroyer but floating between the barges. The balloons, which were really flexible pontoons, were patented jointly by Robertson and their co-inventor, Thomas. Eventually they had four of these balloons, two with a lifting capacity of 150 tons each, and two with a lifting capacity of 100 tons each. The huge bags were made of 12 thicknesses of canvas securely joined with rubber solution. The length of the large balloons when inflated was 47 feet 10 inches.

Wires passing round the envelope were joined at four points six inches apart to the H girder keel. The deflated weight of each balloon was 25 cwt. The 100-ton lifting balloons had their wires gathered at two suspension points. They were fitted with valves which automatically cut off the air when the balloons were fully inflated.

There were no rocks where the destroyers lay, but divers working below found conditions difficult, for though it was a safe anchorage for ships, it was a diver's nightmare because of mud on the bottom which every movement stirred up into an inky mass that blurred their vision.

But before Robertson had lifted his first destroyer, a rival appeared in the person of a Mr Cox who, on 10 January 1924, accompanied by his wife, visited Stromness, looked over the scuttled ships where they lay and examined the land around Lyness. In answer to local enquiries he said he had bought upwards of 20 small craft in addition to *Seydlitz* and *Hindenburg*, and that Lyness had been placed at his disposal together with all available plant. The Admiralty promptly declared that the statement was premature, but in February confirmation was given, and the Annual Register of 1924 records that a contract for the work of salvaging German ships was agreed between the Admiralty and the firm of Cox & Danks, Cox's tender having been lower than those of several larger concerns, one of them a powerful American syndicate.

It is believed that the destroyers on the bottom were sold by the Admiralty on behalf of the Inter-Allied Reparations Committee for about £250 each, one condition of the contract being that the sea-bed where each ship had lain was to be left free of all obstructions. It is presumed that these conditions were modified for the final phase of the operations after World War II when the last few remaining ships had their bottoms blown open so that they could be gutted of anything quickly accessible and profitable, especially of non-radioactive steel.

In April Cox installed listening-sets, cinematograph and other equipment at Lyness for the entertainment in their leisure time of a large work force to be employed by the new firm.

Ernest Frank Guelph Cox, whose salvage work was soon to give him a world-wide reputation, was born in 1883, the 11th child of a Wolverhampton master-draper. At the age of seven he attended Dudley Free School, Wolverhampton, leaving at 13 to become errand boy to a draper. From his youth he was interested in everything mechanical, and particularly in electrical matters on which he obtained books from the Mechanics Institute Library. He came from a modest home. He was a forceful man, often violent and intemperate in speech, and with an unshakable belief in himself, though in administrative matters he was by no means a genius. He left the draper's for a job in a generating station. At the age of 20 he applied successfully to the Corporation of Ryde in the Isle of Wight for the post of chief engineer in charge of a new installation at Lymington in Hampshire. Next he became an assistant engineer at Hamilton in Scotland where he was concerned with the application of industrial power. This was followed by a post as chief engineer to Wishaw Corporation in Lanarkshire where he gained the respect of the local council and married the daughter of a councillor who was proprietor of the Overton Steel Works. He joined this firm as a partner and reorganised it.

He had known from the first what kind of work he wanted, and he applied his considerable powers of concentration and memory to the acquisition of knowledge concerning the use of power in industry. His quick temper, strong language and outspoken remarks earned him the dislike of many people, but he is said to have borne no malice. He worked his men hard, but he seems to have been popular with them, for he knew them all, spoke their language, was constantly among them and was always sensitive about safety precautions. He had courage, too, both moral and physical. When on one occasion he was injured by a baulk of timber falling across his legs, he insisted upon being carried about the wreck until that particular job was finished. At times he was stubborn to the point of foolhardiness, as, for example, in his Scapa Flow operations when an expensive derrick was wrecked because in the face of all expert advice he insisted upon a cable being stretched beyond its breaking point.

Five years after joining the Overton Steel Works, Cox left to set up in partnership with Thomas Danks, his wife's cousin. Danks provided the money. Cox the knowledge and drive. The new firm of Cox & Danks accepted contracts in 1913 and, when war broke out the following year, it began to make shell cases, which provided Cox with sufficient capital to enable him to buy out his partner. At the time of the armistice he was in sole control of a prosperous business equipped with plant and machinery. In 1921 he turned to shipbreaking, and bought for £25,000 each the old battleships *Orion* of 22,500 tons displacement and *Erin* of 23,000 tons. He had these towed to Queensborough, on the Isle of Sheppey in the mouth of the Thames, where he opened a yard. In this yard lay a dock with a lifting capacity of 3,000 tons, surrendered by Germany as part of the reparations for the scuttling of the fleet. Cox bought it from the Admiralty for £24,000. On its floor was a huge steel cylinder used by the Germans for testing the hulls of submarines. It was 400 feet in length and 40 feet in diameter. The method employed was to sink the dock with the submarine sealed inside the cylinder, and then to apply external pressure to the hull. This cylinder projected several feet above the high retaining walls. Otto Willer-Petersen, founder of Petersen & Albeck of Copenhagen, a Danish firm which was a principal buyer of Cox's scrap-metal, suggested that, after the cylinder had been removed from the dock and sold, the dock itself might be used very profitably in the salvage of enemy destroyers in Scapa Flow. At this time Cox expected to be running out of work soon, so he considered the suggestion, at first somewhat doubtfully as he had never before lifted a ship.

The main object of a floating dock is to raise ships out of the water to enable inspection, painting and repair to be undertaken of their underwater parts. The modern floating dock is evolved from the method first devised by an English captain in Cronstadt harbour during the reign of Peter the Great. This man gutted an old hulk, fitted a watertight gate at its stern, berthed his ship in the hollow shell, closed the gate and pumped out the water. It was not until 1785 that a timber dock was built specially for the purpose by Christopher Watson at Rotherhithe.

The floating dock has hollow walls and bottom, and the most common type is the double-sided dock such as Cox bought. As the floating dock itself needs to be lifted out of water for periodical maintenance and is generally too wide to enter a fixed dry dock, it is usually so designed that it can lift every part of itself in turn out of the water.

The main functions of the dock walls are to provide stability when there is no ship on it, to contain the lifting machinery, to form platforms from which to berth the ship and to provide longitudinal strength. The horizontal portion, or pontoon, of the dock is the platform on which the ship rests, and it provides the buoyancy which raises the ship from the water. The pontoon is subdivided by watertight bulkheads to ensure stability. and the walls are also divided.

The basic principle upon which the floating dock works is that for every ton of weight removed from it, the dock itself exerts an upward pressure of an equivalent amount. Centrifugal pumps are therefore installed as low down as possible in the pontoon and worked by prime movers on top of the walls. As the pumps throw out water, so the ship gradually rises.

As yet Cox had not fully assessed the problem of raising these ships which must inevitably have suffered considerable damage by the pressure of water and years of submersion. To some extent his problem was simplified by their reduction to scrap when raised. The essence of his plan was to utilise the buoyancy of his dock and the lift of the tide to raise the sunken vessels clear of the bottom.

The work was not commenced, of course, without at least a rough estimate of the value of the scrap that would result from the operations. Calculations could be based upon the known general structural arrangements of warships, even though drawings and plans of the German ships had not at that time been obtained by Cox. It was known, for example, that many fixtures and fittings and minor portions of the hull were made of aluminium alloy or other light materials, and high-tensile steels were in general use for important parts. Cast steel was used for the stern, stern frame, rudder frame, hawspipes etc, wrought iron for cables, davits and similar fittings, and naval brass, gunmetal or phosphor bronze for many internal fittings. Cox claimed that he could distinguish with his eyes shut all kinds of metal by merely listening to someone tapping it.

The cruiser had two distinct bottoms; the outer bottom forming the outside of the hull transmitted water pressure to the general structure, while the function of the inner one, which was also watertight, was to save the ship should the outer bottom become unserviceable. The outer bottom was one inch thick near the keels and behind the outer protective plating at the sides, and rather less on the bilge. The inner bottom was thinner. The space between the two could be utilised for the stowage of oil fuel and reserve feed water. Systems of frames connected the two bottoms, certain of them being made watertight in order to subdivide the bottom into a number of cells useful for stowage purposes and also limit the inflow of the sea should the outer bottom be damaged. The upper deck was steel plating supported by transverse beams and longitudinal girders. Watertight compartments were provided by watertight bulkheads and decks.

In principle, battleships and battlecruisers were built in the same way, though the plating was thicker and the scantlings heavier. Bulkheads supported the several decks down to the inner bottom where water pressure transmitted through the framing balanced the loads. In the cruisers, armour formed part of the structure, but in the battleships and battlecruisers it consisted of separate hard plates bolted to the sides of the ship.

The destroyer had no double bottom, and the important framing was more closely spaced, the lower part being adapted to support boilers and engines because of the disproportionate weight of machinery these ships carried. The longitudinal frames stiffened the thin plating of special quality steel which in places amidships was as thin as 0.17 inches.

Cox could learn from naval architects about the structure of warships – he had already broken up two battleships – and so form some idea of the difficulties he might encounter. For example, in all classes of warships, damage below the waterline could at best make a ship inoperable were it not for an efficient system of watertight subdivision. Fairly minute subdivision, too, is necessary to minimise danger from shell fragments or accidents which might perforate the hull. By such means, and by making every deck and flat watertight, ships like *Seydlitz* and *von der Tann* had been able to keep on fighting though holed in several places. Even so, damage could still cause a ship to heel or trim to an extent which would affect her manoeuvrability, or prevent her guns from being fired. To correct this, suitable components on the opposite side or end of the ship were flooded, a method used by Cox when ships tended to list during their lift and were in danger of turning over and sinking. Main transverse bulkheads were as far as possible not pierced by doors or any other fittings except essential electric leads and power pipes which were arranged above the waterline.

At the suggestion of an Admiralty official whom Cox had approached with a view to buying the scuttled ships, he had, as told, visited Scapa Flow and decided upon purchase, ignoring the Admiralty's official pronouncement that the ships were at such a depth that salvage was out of the question. Under a later contract he also acquired the battleships *Moltke* and *von der Tann*, the battlecruisers *Kaiser* and *Prinzregent Luitpold*, and the light cruiser *Bremse*.

He loaded the floor of his floating dock with a wide variety of salvage equipment, railway lines, trucks and two crane jibs. Workshops and machinery associated with a floating dock were already in the massive side walls. Compressors, generators and any other necessary equipment were installed. Brackets were fitted on the seaward face of the dock to support 6-inch diameter mild steel shafting. On this shaft were mounted ten grooved pulleys with a diameter of 42 inches to take wire hoisting ropes. Ten hand-operated winches positioned along the dock could be worked in single or double gear. At the back of the dock were anchored pulley blocks with six sheaves of 20-inch diameter. Similar blocks were positioned at the moving end. All these could sustain a load of 100 tons. Liftingwire ropes from the winches were passed through the anchored blocks, and then through the moving blocks, the rope being $1\frac{1}{4}$-inch diameter. Single wire ropes $2\frac{3}{8}$-inch diameter, each capable of a lift of 250 tons, were attached to the moving blocks. Attached to the end of each wire was a Lowmore iron stud link chain of $3\frac{1}{2}$-inch diameter. Two stud chains were installed on deck, each with a lift of $7\frac{1}{2}$ tons at a radius of 75 feet. The vertical back structure was sub-divided into offices, powerhouses, workshops and store-rooms. When the long 700-mile tow to Lyness began, £40,000 had been spent on salvage gear.

Much of the salvage and diving equipment was manufactured by the world-famous firm of Siebe Gorman & Co Ltd. Its founder, Augustus Siebe, had invented an 'open' diving dress in 1819 which was worn in conjunction with an air pump. It was based on the principle of the diving bell, and air found its outlet at the edge of the jacket. But if the wearer fell, water rushed into his dress, and unless he was quickly brought to the surface he was in danger of being drowned. The closed diving apparatus developed from this early invention, similar to the Hard Hat worn today, was also invented by Siebe in 1837. This was connected to an air pump, also manufactured by Siebe Gorman & Co. Pressure gauges on the pump indicated the depth at which the diver was working and the pressure of air being supplied. The helmet could be connected with the breastplate, or corselet, by a slight turn; the equipment was made of copper or bronze. An air supply pipe was attached to a non-return inlet valve in the helmet. An air outlet valve fitted to the helmet allowed the diver to control the amount of air in his dress, and thus his degree of buoyancy.

When the diver began work, he adjusted his valve to maintain his equilibrium. In those days there were no self-contained breathing outfits, and skin-diving had yet to come. The thick glass window fitted to the helmet often steamed over. To clear the mist, the diver had to open the top of a small tube, the spitcock, leading to the outside of the helmet, take a quick mouthful of sea water, then close the tap and squirt the water over the misted glass.

Attached to the helmet was a telephone, also introduced by Siebe Gorman & Co. The receiver was in the crown of the helmet and the wires embedded in the life-line. Unfortunately, the procedure for clearing mist usually shorted the telephone contacts and put them out of action.

The dress itself was made of rubberised twill. It covered the whole body from foot to neck, and the sleeves had vulcanised rubber cuffs to provide a watertight joint at the wrists.

The flexible air-pipe, which passed under the left armpit, had to be stout enough to withstand being cut on sharp edges of metal, and it was always liable to be trapped by a fall. Then there was the life-line for use in an emergency, for hauling the diver to the surface, and for signalling by a certain number of pulls or jerks according to a prearranged code.

The diver's dress was completed by a heavy pair of boots weighted up to 16 pounds each; these enabled him to keep upright in water. He also wore a 40-pound lead weight on his back and another on his chest to enable him to preserve his equilibrium.

Two Admiralty tugs to further the work were bought by Cox and named *Ferrodanks* and *Sidonian*. The captain of *Ferrodanks* had been in Orkney for most of the war carrying water from Stromness to the British fleet.

The floating dock, having completed its long journey to Scapa Flow, was beached at Mill Bay near Lyness. Cox then had one of the great side walls cut away so that chains could be let down over the edge of the platform. As lift would be required from both sides, the dock was cut in two, thus providing two L-shaped docks, each 200 feet in length and 40 feet in width. Each dock was furnished with 12 sets of lifting gear, and each set had a three-gear hand winch and a 100-ton five-sheaved pulley block. It also had five main compartments which could be pumped out separately or joined by means of bulkhead valves. The docks were practically complete power stations. About 65 per cent of the power was generated by dynamos driven by high-speed steam engines, the remaining power being generated by dynamos coupled to, or belt-driven from, internal combustion engines. Eight sets of 6-inch pumps of submersible type were each connected to the machinery room in the dock wall by 100-foot flexible cables covered with rubber sheathing. Power was generated by a 70 kilowatt steam-driven generator set. There was also a 100 brake horsepower direct current motor coupled by a belt to a 60 kilovolt ampère 3-phase generator designed for 50-cycle current at 220 volts. Alternating current was used for working the pumps which were run alternately in pairs. A small 40-cubic-foot compressor was used for the pneumatic tools.

Cox now had the men and the equipment, but everything depended upon team-work, and to that he always paid tribute. The divers, in particular, worked long hours cheerfully, and often in conditions which today would be considered intolerable. Their work was both hard and dangerous, and in those days it was not appreciated that years of diving could affect a man's heart. One diver, Hall, died in his suit; another. 'Busy' Bee, a man perhaps too old for this type of work, died after getting out of one; a third, much later in the operations, after an escape from a nasty situation, was found drowned a few days later though a good swimmer; the diver, James Thomson, who worked on nine of the capital ships raised, and H. Murray Taylor, a salvage officer, were both awarded the MBE for dangerous work successfully accomplished in attaching wires to two live torpedoes which had not been fully discharged from a submarine.

An average man could dive to five fathoms. If his physical condition was good he could descend to ten fathoms. Deeper than that extreme fitness was necessary, while at 20 fathoms only those exceptionally fit could endure the conditions to which the body was subjected. Divers encountered poisonous and explosive gases in the ships. Their air-pipes were liable to be cut on a sharp edge or trapped by a fall. There were the hazards of marine life, too: Harry Grosset was badly bitten on the hand by a conger eel while pushing an air-pipe through a porthole. Conger eels were everywhere. Trapped in a cabin, a grey seal died and was used to play a frightening practical joke upon a new nervous diver. White-faced, the man rushed up to the salvage officer and gasped that a dead sailor lay in a bunk in *Hindenburg's* cabin. Told that such a thing was impossible, he took the salvage officer down to prove his story, and there lay the dead seal dressed by the man's workmates in sailor's clothing, its tail end covered with a blanket. In one of the destroyers a very large lobster which must have been five or six years old had taken up its home in one of the compartments which it defended vigorously with outsize claws whenever anyone attempted to enter it. T. McKenzie, the chief salvage officer, related an occasion when, inspecting an upturned destroyer at a depth of some 30 feet, he thought another vessel was almost upon him. He flattened himself under the wreck, and soon afterwards a terrific jerk on his breast-rope tore him out, free and unharmed. Then he saw that his near accident had been caused by the flick of a 40-foot whale's tail. Schools of playful whales became such a nuisance for a time that all divers were called up as soon as they were seen in the vicinity.

As far as possible workers were obtained locally. These trained others on the job, divers especially. The old divers welcomed recruits as the recruit's first successful dive ended in 'drinks all round'. But Cox's most valuable find was his young salvage officer, T. McKenzie, who had been educated at Glasgow High School and had qualified as a member of the Scottish Institute of Civil Engineers. His father, under whom he had obtained his experience and learned how to dive, was a sea captain, the only one in Scotland experienced in salvage work. Among young McKenzie's varied tasks he had spent two years in the search for a Spanish treasure ship, though only a few pieces-of-eight were found. After enlarging his experience with the Glasgow Trust, he qualified as a member of the Institute of Mechanical Engineers. Another contract took him on salvage work off the West African coast, and it was upon his return in 1923, when he was a foreman diver on the Clyde, that he made the acquaintance of Cox whilst on holiday, through a mutual interest in fresh-water fishing. Cox had just obtained additional financial aid for his salvage venture and, having an eye for a good man, he persuaded McKenzie to work for him. This was the beginning of a brilliant career in salvage work. Cox provided the money and the drive, but without McKenzie's imagination and technical ability the German fleet might never have been raised. Cox began by engaging about 20 technicians of different skills from Sheerness dockyard, and about the same number from Aberdeen and Glasgow. When work got into its stride he had a labour force of about 200 men. They lived in the old naval camp he had bought at Lyness and speedily evolved their own class distinctions. The aristocracy of the workers, the divers and their mates, lived together in huts; mechanics formed the next group in the social scale, living together in their huts, and lastly the labourers in theirs. These distinctions were jealously preserved. It was almost a womanless world, for there was no married accommodation. At no one time were there more than four wives living at Lyness, the senior of them being Mrs McKenzie, the wife of the young chief salvage officer, who was to spend 24 years in all at Scapa Flow. The main social functions were the dances, and later, when Metal Industries Ltd took over, the banquets after each successful lift.

Cox soon discovered that the Orcadians had been before him. In the tradition of their old Viking forebears they had carried out some unauthorised salvage work on their own account. With the gay abandon of the *karate* team which recently demolished a derelict house with bare hands, the fishermen, with scarcely more equipment, had removed thousands of pounds worth of fittings and metal, including a number of gun-metal torpedo tubes then worth £100 each – in fact, anything which could be reached and moved. A few of them had also gone out to *Seydlitz*, alongside which they had sunk their fishing-boat so that it could not be seen by patrols or watchmen, and had lived aboard while stripping her down to water-level of all brass, gun-metal and copper. On *Hindenburg* all metal of any value above water had vanished: electricity cables, telephone wiring gear, switches, lamps and even removable brass screws had been smuggled away in barrels labelled 'herrings'. When Cox decided that the time had come to employ watchmen of his own, he advertised in the local newspaper, and one of the applicants, as a testimony to his knowledge of the ships, stated that he had kept watch for the men who had stripped them. Yet these were the same Orcadians upon whom their future employers could never lavish high enough praise for their loyalty, endurance, courage, skill and resource, and close ties between many of them and the then chairman of Metal Industries Ltd, the firm which virtually ended the work of salvage, still exist.

'Marine salvage is the term generally applied to the saving of ships and cargoes from loss or partial loss by wreck, whether due to storm or tempest, fire, collision, enemy action etc. The term is equally applicable to the saving of flotsam and jetsam and to the payment made to salvors by way of awards for services rendered.' This definition prefaced a paper written by T. McKenzie, who was the man most closely connected with practically the whole of the work in raising the scuttled German fleet. His definition must in this case be modified to the extent that the sunken vessels were sold by the Admiralty to the salvors who then made what profit they could from the deal.

6

The Destroyers

THE DESTROYERS, AS LISTED by von Reuter in his book *Scapa Flow – Das Grab der deutscher Flotte* (The Grave of the German Fleet) are shown at Appendix 4.

V70, upright in only 50 feet of water, was an obvious first choice for lifting. She had a standard displacement of 924 tons and lay only half a mile from Lyness where Cox had bought the abandoned naval camp and air station in which his men were accommodated.

The usual method adopted by marine salvage companies when using pontoons or lifting craft was to pin them to the wreck at low water and use the rising tide as a lifting agent, the wreck being beached again and repinned at successive low tides. The lifting of ships, however, was something new to Cox, and his mind was receptive to any idea which seemed practicable. The scheme evolved by McKenzie was new, but it commended itself to Cox and he decided to try it.

So much had already been spent on equipment that Cox decided to use the cables and 3-inch chains from his own enormous stock rather than buy great quantities of new 9-inch circumference steel-wire rope.

In March 1924 the two docks, which were in reality floating platforms, were moored on either side of *V70*. Lifting chains were placed in position under the destroyer's hull by divers working in pairs on each side of the vessel. But first the stern had to be raised by wires under the propeller shaft to get the lifting chains into position.

At low water the sea level fell from ten to 12 feet at spring tides. In theory, therefore, if the slack of the lifting-wires was taken up, *V70* would be lifted by the rising tide ten feet from the bottom without the use of any other mechanical aid. Then the ship could be towed into shallower water, and the whole process repeated as often as was necessary until the wreck was beached. The use of hand-winches increased the height to which the ship could be lifted from the bottom. The load on the pulley blocks could be estimated roughly by the number of men it took to wind the hand-winches. Four meant they had a safe load, but six indicated an unacceptable degree of danger. Lowmore chains were used for lifting. At the end of each chain was a hook, and this was made fast to any hole in the hull or the superstructure.

The preliminary work was completed in ten days. Three or four ropes were adequate for raising the stern. Further ropes placed under the ship's bottom were so arranged that, as the ship was carried from deep to shallower water, their length could be altered conveniently as required. With this in view, they were divided into different lengths connected by large shackles. When necessary, divers bored small tunnels under the ship and passed 'messenger' wires through them to which the lifting-wires could be attached and drawn under the wreck. The method is illustrated in Figure 1.

Sea conditions were ideal on the Saturday evening preceding the attempted lift. At the close of day, all the hawsers were hauled tight, leaving the bow above water. The final operations began on Sunday morning, but when the destroyer was seven feet clear of the bottom, the load was so great that the hooks tore through the steelwork and the docks heeled inwards with the weight. Suddenly one of the 3-inch chains snapped under the load, the first of all but two as the lifting gear exploded in all directions and flew about like shrapnel. The sound was described by one of the salvage officers as being like an artillery bombardment. Happily no one had been injured, though 25 men had been working on each pontoon.

In this condition it was considered unsafe to lower the dock

Method of straight lift

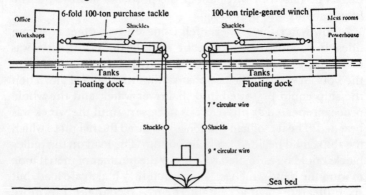

Method of sideways lift

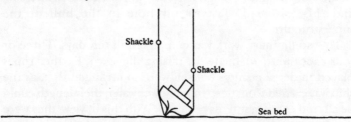

Figure 1. Arrangements of ropes for lifting destroyers.

and destroyer into shallow water, so the winches were run back and the ship allowed to sink, and a few minutes later 100 workmen were putting on their coats and being taken in *Ferrodanks* to Lyness. This was an instance where Cox had ignored the advice of his salvage staff. Just as a walking stick can support as much from its handle as the holder can raise in a vertical lift but will break easily when snapped across the knee, so the giant links easily took the load of the upward lift but broke when bent over the small pulley winches. Cox had received an expensive lesson. Some of the workmen described the chains as having snapped like carrots.

New 9-inch steel-wire ropes with a breaking strain of 250 tons were obtained from Glasgow. These were flat wire slings 15 inches broad which were passed under the hull to form a cradle. The dock was prepared for a fresh lift, and at 16.00 hrs on 31 July 1924 the second attempt was made at dead low tide. Ninety-

Top *Kronprinz Wilhelm* followed by *Markgraf* off the coast of Scotland at the surrender of the German High Seas fleet to Admiral Beatty. (*Illustrated London News*)

Centre The German fleet in Scapa Flow. In the foreground is part of Mainland showing army camps and the boom defence. Cava is middle centre with Fara behind it and on the horizon the island of Hoy. (*C. Patterson*)

Below Panoramic view of Scapa Flow showing the normal anchorage of the British fleet, on which has been superimposed the position of the scuttled German ships. The heavy ships are in two lines in the Bring Deeps off Houton Head, and the light craft chiefly between Cava Island and Hoy. *Baden* lies aground in Swanbister Bay, top centre. (*The Sphere*)

Bernard Gribble's drawing made from the deck of the captured German ship *Sochos* showing at extreme left *König Albert* heeling over, *Bayern*, centre background behind boats, *Grosser Kurfürst* on right, and in right background the light cruiser *Emden*.

chosins's crew are driving back two boatloads of Germans who were trying to force
eir way aboard. (*Illustrated London News*)

Top German destroyer capsizing after having been scuttled. (*The Sphere*)
Centre *Bayern* sinking by stern after having been scuttled. (*Shipbreaking Industries*)
Below Destroyers sinking and beached on the island of Fara. (*C. Patterson*)

Above The Last *Kamerad* of World War 1. German sailors approaching HMS *Revenge* after abandoning their sinking ship. (*The Sphere*)

Below A coaling boat stuck on one of the sunken ships which until raised were a danger to navigation. (*J. Robertson*)

Above Sinking of *Hindenburg*—phase 1. The forward compartments have flooded rapidly through she is still more or less on an even keel. (*The Sphere*)

Below Sinking of *Hindenburg*—phase 3. With the flooding of other compartments, the ship has righted herself. Only her forward superimposed turret and superstructure are now above water. Beyond the guns is the light cruiser, *Nürnberg*, which lies beached on Cava Island. (*The Sphere*)

Above Sinking of *Hindenburg*—phase 2. One of the screws begins to show as she lists heavily. (*The Sphere*)

Below Sinking of *Hindenburg*—phase 4. *Hindenburg* has settled on the bottom, her masts, funnels and the upper part of her superstructure and upper gun turret showing. (*The Sphere*)

Above The vast bulk of the floating dock passes under the Forth Bridge on its way from Rosyth. (*Shipbreaking Industries*)

Centre One of the four destroyers lifted by the Scapa Flow Salvage and Shipbreaking Co. The destroyers were raised by inflating balloons on either side of the wreck and by the use of concrete barges. (*Illustrated London News*)

Bottom A view of another destroyer lifted by the same company, showing the balloons on either side of the weed–encrusted hull. (*C. Patterson*)

Jimmy Thomas, a diver responsible for much of the successful salvage work. (*Conway Picture Library*)

A diver fully equipped in the Siebe-Gorman diving-suit. (*Siebe, Gorman & Co*)

Two Cox & Danks divers and their assistants about to examine a wreck. (*J.Robertson*)

Right One of the heavy lifting chains that broke during the first attempt to raise destroyer *V70*. (*Illustrated London News*)

Below *V70*, the first destroyer to be lifted, between the floating docks. The winches and the 9-in and 10-in wire lifting-ropes made the salvage possible. (*A. S. Thomson*)

Left *Hindenburg*, easily recognisable by her great tripod mast, listing before the main mooring wire snapped, letting her capsize. (*C. Patterson*)

Below *Hindenburg* between the floating docks with tugs in attendance. (*C. Patterson*)

Above *Hindenburg* approaching maximum list between the floating docks. The mooring wires have snapped and she is about to sink again. (*C. Patterson*)

Below Here she is surrounded by cranes and salvage craft before one of the unsuccessful attempts to float her. (*Illustrated London News*)

Left The first air-lock being towed out to *Hindenburg*. (*Shipbreaking Industries*)

Below Air-locks being fixed in position. The tug, *Sidonian*, is to the right of the pontoon. Workmen are climbing the ladders to enter the locks.
(*Shipbreaking Industries*)

Above *Moltke* passing under the Forth Bridge on her way to Rosyth. In the picture are two of the three German tugs which had such a rough passage with her in the Pentland Firth.(*Illustrated London News*)

Below Salvage work on *Moltke*. A tall air-lock has been replaced by a short one on the right for the entrance of workmen into the upturned hull. In the background is a tug supplying compressed air. (*Illustrated London News*)

Above *Moltke* on tow in a rough sea. Between the small air-locks which replaced the tall ones is the hut in which the crew were accommodated. The towing vessel is near the horizon far right. (*Shipbreaking Industries*)

Below *Moltke* in dry dock at Rosyth. Her great propeller tubes are ready for removal. (*Illustrated London News*)

Last voyage of *Hindenburg* taken from the Forth Bridge. The huts on deck were living accommodation for the crew during the voyage. This was the only capital ship not lifted upside down. (*R. W. McCrone*)

Above The keel of *Seydlitz* above water. Mid-centre, like a tilted funnel, is an air-lock. (C. Patterson)

Left *Seydlitz* on tow to Rosyth, showing the hand-winches and the hut in which members of the salvage crew were accommodated. (*A. S. Thomson*)

Below *Seydlitz* on tow. Earlier, Cox had attached a destroyer to the stanchions, middle left, in an attempt to keep *Seydlitz* from listing. (*Shipbreaking Industries*)

Right *Seydlitz* on tow in a rough sea. (*A. S. Thompson*)

Below *Kaiser* on tow with *Ferrodanks* and German tugs—stern view. (*Ship-breaking Industries*)

Above *Von der Tann* passing under the Forth Bridge on her way to be broken up at Rosyth. (*Norval*)

Below *Von der Tann* being towed into the lock at Rosyth. (*The Scotsman*)

Above The bells of *Derfflinger* and *Friedrich der Grosse* which were returned to Germany. (*Zentrales Marinekommando*)
Below Captain Steffan and Admiral Erdmann at Wilhelmshaven on September 3 1965 when the two bells and the seal of *Derfflinger* arrived in Germany after their presentation to the German navy at Faslane Port. (*Zentrales Marinekommando*)

Above *Derfflinger's* seal, found by one of the workers, which was returned to Germany. (*Zentrales Marinekommando*)

Below Bow of *Prinzregent Luitpold* breaking surface, showing some of her 40-foot and 60-foot air-locks. (*A.S. Thomson*)

Above *Prinzregent Luitpold*, keel uppermost, under the Forth Bridge near the end of her last voyage. (*Shipbreaking Industries*)

Below Stern view of *Prinzregent Luitpold* in dock at Rosyth. The breaking up is well advanced. The successive deck levels can be seen, also the method of blocking up the ship. (*The Scotsman*)

Above *Bertha*, the salvage vessel, standing off one of the wrecks from which escaping air is rising. (*J. Robertson*)

Below *Bertha* and *Metinda*, salvage tugs, moored to a wreck. (*Associated Scottish Newspapers*)

Bertha, the tug which played a prominent part in the salvage operations. Originally she belonged to Southern Railways and sailed between Channel ports. After her purchase by Metal Industries she was converted at Grangemouth into a salvage vessel. (*Star Photos*)

six men began to turn the 24 winch handles. The sea was calm. Inch by inch, aided also by the tide, *V70* rose from the sea-bed until she was only two feet below water, the whole of her upperworks being visible at high water. Like all wrecks subsequently raised, the bright incrustations of marine growth soon became a dirty brown and began to stink, yet there had been little rusting. Four similar lifts were made at successively shallower depths before *V70* could be beached on a sandbank at Mill Bay on the Saturday morning, just ten years after the declaration of war. She survived an uncomfortable night's tow in a howling gale to Lyness. The lifting and beaching had occupied only a little more than seven hours though, because of the mishap with chains, the whole operation had been spread over six weeks. This time it had proceeded so smoothly that not a hammer or a spanner had been needed during the lift which had been performed solely by turning the winch handles.

Then it was discovered that pirate divers had stripped the destroyer of her gun-metal torpedo tubes and everything else which could be lifted. Moreover the price of scrap had slumped unexpectedly from £5 to about £1 15s per ton so, instead of reducing *V70* to scrap, Cox made her hull watertight, pumped her dry, renamed her *Salvage Unit No 3*, and used her as a floating workshop.

The next destroyer selected for lifting lay on her side. As only the middle portion rested on the bottom, it was relatively easy to pass ropes under the fore and aft portions. To begin with six ropes were passed under the stern, and as these were wound up, additional ropes were passed through, 12 being found sufficient for the ship to be towed ashore. But the problem was how to turn the destroyer into a vertical position so that she could be lifted into the narrow opening between the two platforms. She was therefore towed into deeper water. Then the pulley-blocks were paid out on one side and wound up on the other and by this method, which was followed in subsequent operations where a ship was not vertical, a destroyer could easily be turned over in a single morning. If, however, it was completely upside down, resting on its bridge and forward gun, ropes could be passed under the hull, most of which was six feet from the bottom, and the vessel turned after two days' work. The first destroyer was raised in a total of 12 days' work; the third destroyer took only six days, while the last was raised in only four days. It became a familiar sight: the panting, powerful tugs, the great towering walls of the dock with a wreck between them, its hull so encrusted with marine growths of every kind that the bridge could not be distinguished from the gun platform or the forecastle from the after deck, resembling a submarine reef more than a ship.

Some of the destroyers were more than 300 feet long, while the salvage platforms were only 240 feet. Sometimes their position over the destroyers was misjudged, but on the whole the work proceeded smoothly, though the diver's work was always hard and dangerous. A.S. Thomson recalled how divers had frequently surfaced in such a tangle of air and life-lines that it reminded one of a cat playing with a ball of string.

At first divers used hacksaws to cut mooring ropes from destroyers when lashed together, but on one occasion, as this released the load on the severed ropes, the upward rush of freed metal knocked the diver off his feet and a giant mooring buoy shot out of the water bearing with it a heavy anchor chain.

Only one flame cutting tool, a French one, was effective at depths greater than 15 feet, so McKenzie began to use gelignite charges when ropes had to be severed.

Meanwhile Robertson had been running into trouble with his attempts at balloon lifts. A spirit of rivalry had grown between the two competing salvage teams, but Cox was lifting his third destroyer on 29 August 1924, the day when Robertson lifted his first. This was the only occasion on which two ships were raised on the same day.

Robertson's destroyer was *S131* on which preliminary work by a salvage gang of a dozen men had taken two months. The United Kingdom Salvage Company was associated with Robertson's company in this attempt. The destroyer's masts were removed to obviate interference with the lifting gear. One funnel had disappeared and others were badly dented. The little gun on the foredeck was in a state of decay and covered with weeds. The 'camels', or balloons, were inflated by a compressor on one of the barges after they had been submerged and attached to the vessel. The tackle consisted of 16 10-inch wire belts attached to 5-inch wire hawsers which in turn were shackled to $1\frac{1}{2}$-inch cables. The Lowmore iron chains were hand-forged and were carried with pulleys to $2\frac{3}{4}$-inch screws operated by powerful spanners. Thus each of the eight sets of girders had double lifting tackle consisting of 16 belts, 32 wire hawsers and 32 chain cables. The breaking load of the chains was 65 tons, and of the belts 100 tons, which provided an ample safety margin. As the balloons were inflated *S131* gradually rose, and the more orthodox lifting tackle was then brought into use to relieve the strain. The hawsers had been made tight at low water, and when the tide had risen 12 feet, which further assisted the lift, *Trustee*, in a stiffish breeze and a slight ground swell, towed Robertson's first prize shorewards.

Cox's work proceeded more rapidly. Some labour trouble arose during the lift of the fifth destroyer when certain employees needed for manning the winches had to return home to help with the harvest. However, the crew of the Longhope lifeboat took their places and the work went on. While Cox was well advanced with work on his sixth destroyer, the Scapa flow Salvage Co were gradually moving their second ship, but operations were delayed by the bursting of one of the balloons. On 13 November 1924 Robertson successfully lifted his third ship and began work on his fourth and last, while Cox suspended operations until winter was over. Shortly before this Cox had suffered an accident during the erection on the pier of a large electric crane, but he soon recovered.

In December Robertson secured his barges to the destroyer and, though salvage work was slow in the dull short days, he successfully raised the ship. In the following month, on 22 January 1925, he suffered some financial loss when a severe gale dragged the anchors of his concrete barges, landing them high and dry and giving him considerable trouble before they were floated away. Incidentally, they had been built of concrete because of the shortage of metal at the time.

Cox now had the fleet to himself, but on 22 April 1925 fire broke out on the ex-German floating dock which had enough explosives in her store to have blown her sky-high but for the prompt action of T. McKenzie, who was assisted by Carmichael, one of the divers. The ninth destroyer had been successfully lifted, and a fireman was banking the furnace for the next shift and cleaning out the ashes. As usual, the sea around the destroyer was covered with a thick deposit of oil. The fireman thoughtlessly threw a shovelful of hot ashes into the sea through an opening in the dock. The oil burst into flame and the fire spread rapidly, enveloping the dock in a sea of flames. The working party was hurriedly recalled as it was leaving after the day's work, but their efforts would have been unavailing but for McKenzie's presence of mind. Within three minutes he brought into action a submersible pump with which he extinguished the fire. Although the workshops on the lifting dock were badly burned, the lifting gear suffered only slight damage and work was soon back to normal.

In June the first fatal accident occurred. Donald Henderson, one of the labourers, was killed by the collapse of an electric crane when its jib fell upon him. Henderson had worked 18 hours on the Wednesday, 18 hours on Thursday and had begun work again at 16.00 hours on Friday, the day of his death. The crane had been run continuously for 35 hours, but no fault had been found with it, all routine inspections had been carried out, and a jury found no blame attributable to anyone.

By the beginning of 1925 six destroyers had been raised, seven were lying on their sides in 60 feet of water, and several which had been beached lay in a vertical position on the sea bottom. Preparations were already in hand for raising more ships, and a second and larger floating dock was bought. In this dock, which had walls 40 feet high, a large central opening about 30 feet wide and 36 feet high was cut in the end wall so that it could accommodate the bow of a destroyer. It was furnished with eight sets of 6-inch pumps of submersible type manufactured by Submersible Motors Ltd of Southall, and power was generated by a 70-kilowatt Bellis and Morcom steam-driven generator set designed for 220-volt working. It had five main compartments which could either be pumped out separately or joined one to another by bulkhead valves. On Thursday 27 August 1925 the tugs *Plover* and *Homer*, owned by Lawson Batey Ltd of Newcastle-upon-Tyne, took the dock in tow at about 18.30 hours and at high tide brought it clear of Queensborough Pier. The voyage to Lyness took ten days.

Cox intended to use the two smaller docks to manoeuvre the big destroyers on to the floor of the new dock which was to be sunk on to the sea bed and then raised with the wreck.

On the upper part of each dock, hand-winches were set about 20 feet apart. These were provided with 100-ton pulley blocks attached to circular lifting-wires of 9-inch diameter. In order to right a ship, the two docks were again positioned over the sunken vessel. Divers passed the ten ropes from one dock under the hull of the wreck and attached them to pulley blocks on the other dock so that the wreck rested on a cradle of ten lifting-wires. All that was then necessary was to take a weight of 370 tons which was approximately half the wreck's tonnage, and then pay out rope on one set of winches and take it up on the other set. On the paying-out side, the sheaves of blocks were about 20 feet apart to begin with, and 36 feet apart when the ship was righted. The friction between the lifting-ropes and the skin of the ship was sufficient to manoeuvre the wreck gradually, in about six hours, into a vertical position without parbuckling of any kind. (A parbuckle is the purchase formed by a single rope round a heavy object for hoisting or lowering on an inclined plane, the object itself acting as a movable pulley.)

The scuttled destroyers which had been lashed together were now a tangled mass of cables, chains, guns, funnels and masts. These wrecks had to be separated before any attempt at lifting could be made.

The Germans had done their work thoroughly. An inspection of four destroyers disclosed that condenser doors had been removed and that all auxiliary valves, sea connections in boiler rooms and magazine valves had been opened. Hatches and watertight doors had been raised. They had even left unfastened the ports and lavatory connections, and they had removed all the plates which indicated the positions of the various valves they had opened.

Aware that many well-known experts prophesied failure, Cox began lifting more destroyers. By the end of 20 months, 24 had been lifted. In one period of 39 weeks, and without Sunday work, 14 were raised, one of them, *S65*, in the record time of only four days from the commencement of the work. Ten were rendered sufficiently seaworthy to be towed to Rosyth for breaking up by the middle of 1925. Several were sold to shipbreaking firms, and others were dismantled and broken up by Cox & Danks at Lyness. This achievement enabled Cox to recoup half his outlay. By October 1926 only a few bare hulls were to be seen in Mill Bay.

While they had been working on the fourth destroyer an unpleasant accident occurred when a diver went down between two ships which were lashed together, and was trapped by a funnel which had fallen, his only exit being jammed by it. His line was caught, and he could not move. He kept up his spirits by singing *Home, Sweet Home* while other divers managed to secure wires round the funnel so that it could be slung clear, and he was soon released, unharmed by his experience.

Meanwhile, an attempt had been made to manoeuvre the first of the large destroyers, *G103*, into the big floating dock, but the gap between the 40-foot walls was not wide enough to admit the two L-docks with the destroyer between them. So the big dock was beached, one side was removed, and it was towed out again. *G103* was again raised, and this time manoeuvred on to the floor of the big dock and secured to its wall. But the dock keeled over with its weight, and *G103* slid down the sloping deck, one corner of which struck the sea bed. The bottom tanks were flooded, and both dock and destroyer sank to the bottom. Their refloating proved to be one of the most difficult operations with which the salvage team had had to deal, and thereafter Cox used the big dock only as a workshop and as a platform for boilers.

The floating docks were moored over the 11th destroyer, *S65*, on 12 May 1925, and on Saturday 16th she had been lifted in a record time of four days.

After one of the destroyers had been raised, a diver reported that he had found the ship's safe below, and Cox assembled a small party to watch it being opened on deck. Everyone crowded round wondering what items of value could have been locked in it before the ship was scuttled. Cox was the only one not to laugh when the sole object inside it was brought out – a chamber-pot, and this was solemnly presented to Mrs McKenzie, the only lady aboard at the time. Was it the joke of a young high-spirited officer who guessed that eventually the safe would be found? Or was it a last gesture of contempt?

The 13th destroyer, *S32*, took twice as long as its forerunners and the working time occupied nine days, a gale blowing almost from the time the floating docks were moved out. It was after the first 18 had been salved that work began on the seven large 320-foot destroyers.

A simple device to show how far men had winched a ship from the bottom was the attachment of an iron rod to the deck. The rod was marked to show the level when the lift began, and as it emerged during the winching, it could be seen at a glance how far the ship had been winched from the bottom.

five ships were refloated between February and April 1926, the last of them, *G104*, on the last day of the month. In 20 months 23,000 tons had been raised.

While the destroyers were being lifted, the positions of the capital ships had been charted. Those which were completely submersed were located by sweeping. The approximate positions of most ships were known, and an hour's work was usually long enough for a ship in this category to be pinpointed. Then divers descended to fit marker buoys foreward and aft, and a tug was moored in position over the wreck. When *Bertha* was used for this purpose in the latter stages of the operation, eight $7\frac{1}{2}$-ton anchors were needed to hold her in position because of the strong, variable winds encountered in Scapa Flow.

7

Hindenburg *Fights Back*

WHILE THE DESTROYERS WERE being lifted, plans were well advanced for raising *Hindenburg*, a battlecruiser built between July 1913 and the middle of 1917. She was one of the three battlecruisers of the *Derfflinger* class, the only battlecruisers at the time of their completion to carry 12-inch guns, superimposed turrets and tripod masts, and to be flush-decked. Many experts considered these ships to be the best capital ships of their time.

Hindenburg, the biggest ship of the fleet, had not taken part in the battle of Jutland. She lay, perfectly upright in 70 feet of water, half a mile west of the island of Cava, apparently presenting Cox with an easy task, though the experts again prophesied failure. Even at this depth, her great tripod mast, her funnels and a good part of her upperworks showed above water. At spring tides her deck was just awash. Ordinarily her flagstaff was almost covered, and nearly 28 feet of water lay over her aft quarter deck. Her huge size and weight made it impossible for her to be raised by the method so successful with destroyers. Cox's original intention was to float her and use her as a pontoon for taking the guns and turrets off *Seydlitz*, and then for raising other vessels.

Various plans for floating her had been investigated. One was a project for raising her by means of air-filled pontoons; another, submitted by a German firm of salvage engineers, involved freezing up all deck apertures and then using compressed air to expel the imprisoned water. Both were rejected in favour of Cox & Danks' own ideas.

The big dock, like the first one, was cut in two, and each part was fitted with workshops complete with generators, pumps, compressors and diving equipment, besides kitchens and mess rooms.

Cox and McKenzie went down in diving suits to make their first survey of *Hindenburg*. It was decided to patch all the holes in her hull, position dock sections on each side, raise her by pumping out the water from her hull so that she could be lifted by her own buoyancy, and then to moor her to the four sections of the floating docks for her tow to the breakers.

They had a stroke of luck when some of the plans of the ship were found in the control room, despite the fact that one of the divers said he had examined the ship for documents without success three weeks after she had been scuttled. Among plans now discovered was the pumping plan which showed the arrangement and positions of the control points for each valve. This enabled four experienced divers to examine the controls of all the valves which could not be reached from outside. They carried down no submersible lighting, for it would not have penetrated the inky darkness caused by mud and particles stirred up when they moved. Everything had therefore to be done by touch.

Sixteen divers were employed, working in pairs. Sometimes they, too, had to work in darkness by touch, at other times by Siebe Gorman submersible lights operated from the docks. They reported that all *Hindenburg*'s open sea valves were so damaged that they could not be closed again. One diver said that when he was lowered into the ship, it looked like a vast submarine forest because of the density of marine growths, and for a time he did not know where he was. He found glasses and champagne bottles strewn about and bunks undisturbed with mattresses still in them.

William Hourston, a local photographer commissioned by *The Times* to take photographs of the ship, had a frightening experience when, five decks down, he saw that he had less than half an inch of candle to light his way back. The flame flickered out just as he dimly saw daylight far above him. On his next descent, to provide against a similar occurrence, he took with him a ball of twine which he unwound as he made his way about the interior.

The most interesting object found was the beautifully executed model of a warship. It was two feet long and showed all the outside structure, deck fittings, gun turrets etc. One room was found clean and dry, without a drop of water in it, after seven years' submersion.

In the summer of 1926 work was stopped temporarily by the great general strike. Two hundred tons of coal were needed weekly for the boilers upon which so much of the equipment depended. The price of coal soared from £1 to £4 15s a ton, well beyond Cox's means at that time as he was paying £1,000 a week in wages and another £1,000 in fuel. However, this time luck was with him, for through the exposed armour-plating of *Seydlitz,* whose side rose above the 65 feet of water in which she lay, they could see that the coal bunkers were full, and they were able to use this coal throughout the strike.

Quick-setting cement was used to seal the damaged bottom valves from inside, and then the openings had to be patched. This was a colossal task as 800 holes had to be patched or plugged and made watertight. Some of the smallest patches were for portholes, and the largest patch was over a hole left by the removal of a badly corroded funnel. This needed a patch 40 feet long by 21 feet wide by six inches thick; it was made ashore and weighed 11 tons. Then it was towed out, lifted by crane on to a dock, lowered into position and used to plug the gaping hole. Five months passed in patching and sealing. Except where wooden plugs could be used, wood planks varying in thickness from one inch to six inches were employed. As the top deck of No 2 turret was just above high water at the spring tides, operations began at that point. All machinery was removed from the centre of the turret and, as the level of the water fell by pumping, all internal obstructions were cut away to give a clear passage right to the bottom of the ship so that it was possible to place submersible pumps at the lowest level.

The sequence of pumping operations had been carefully considered when the work of patching was well advanced. There were two classes of pumping sets, the first being self-contained and driven by oil engines. These comprised several old engine-driven 12-inch *Conqueror* sets built by W.H. Allen, Sons & Co Ltd of Yoker, Glasgow and Lindsay, and by Swan & Hunter Ltd of Newcastle-upon-Tyne. The second class was mainly a series of 20 or more submersible pumps built by Submersible Motors Ltd of Southall. The pumps were connected by cab-tyred sheathed cables to the generating plant on the pontoons, and current was supplied by alternating-current generators driven by belting from steam engines. The steam was supplied by two water-tube boilers.

The 18 pumps which were to be used were connected and tested. On 6 August pumping began, but many of the patches were not watertight. This was no fault of the workmen, for divers discovered that little fish, saith, had acquired a taste for the tallow used with the packing to make the patches watertight, so the tallow was made unpalatable by mixing it with cement.

On the night of 24 August *Hindenburg* was flooded by a gale which drove destroyer *G38*, being used as a breakwater, on to the end of one of the floating docks, pounding it so severely that some plates burst and leakage to a tank was caused. The destroyer had to be removed immediately and the damaged dock repaired, during which time *Hindenburg* had to be completely flooded again. By the end of the month the patches had been re-packed and pumping began again. Considerable time was saved by making a template for each patch, getting the divers to fit it, and then making a patch from the template. The patches were invariably built plank by plank ashore and completed ready for fixing before being sent down. This gave a much closer fit than would have been possible had they been made under water. Between patch and ship was a 'pudding' joint, which was a canvas bag, the pudding, padded with oakum, being lightly nailed round the outer edge of the patch. It was about three inches wide and from two-and-a-half to three inches thick, but when the bolts of the patch were fully tightened, it was squeezed to a thickness of about a quarter of an inch.

It had been assumed that *Hindenburg*'s stern lay on sand and shingle into which it could be forced as the bows were raised, thus providing stability. But in fact the propellers were from ten to 12 feet above solid rock on which the ship lay, and not supporting it as they had expected. It was apparent later that they had been trying to balance *Hindenburg's* 100 feet of width on a keel only three feet wide, for as the days passed, no matter which end was first lifted, *Hindenburg* listed and began to turn over. On the Saturday she suddenly rose 20 feet between 07.00 hrs and 08.00 hrs, her main deck rising well above water and exposing her battery deck, the flagpole on her stern and the starboard quarters. Acting against all advice, Cox decided to maintain the 25,000-ton mass of metal in an upright position by attaching two five-inch steel hawsers from the top of her mast to a destroyer sunk off the island of Cava. As might have been expected, the hawsers snapped like violin strings and once again *Hindenburg* heeled over and went down.

A total of eight 12-inch and 30 six-inch pumps which could discharge 3,600 tons of water per hour were placed aboard. The diving team lashed back the bulkhead doors in the forward compartment so that water could drain towards the stern and bows by their own buoyancy. Otherwise water would have been imprisoned in compartments, upsetting the trim of the ship and creating undue stresses on the hull. Divers had already commented on the heavy corrugation on some hulls due to such pressures. But when pumping began, the rate of fall in the level of water was far less than had been calculated owing to the number of small leaks which now became visible. After four or five months' hard work these were repaired and the bows began to rise. However, the hull had to be flooded again to find new holes through which suction pipes could be passed.

The men were busy aboard lowering the big pumping sets as the water level sank inside the ship. For this to be done, steel deck had to be cut through with oxy-acetylene burners – dangerous work on slimy steel plates. Pumps were kept going night and day, and on the fifth day the bows rose from the depths. Excitement exploded into a great burst of cheering although the men had seen 25 destroyers raised from the sea bed and might well have regarded this as 'just another ship'.

Hindenburg was afloat again when on 2 September a considerable amount of work was undone by a fierce north-westerly gale which, lasting throughout the night, set the dock

rolling and *Hindenburg* heaving. There was trouble with pumps
and dynamos, and the big water-tube boilers broke down. By
their failure the most important and flexible pumping units
were completely deprived of current, while the remaining
pumps were totally inadequate for the task of righting the vessel.
Cox then tried to obtain steam for the engines of the generating
sets from the large tug which was moored alongside the lifting-
pontoon, but because of the poor quality of the foreign coal,
and the ship being stationary, a sufficient head of steam could
not be raised. So many patches had been smashed that
Hindenburg began to sink fast. Another £10,000 had been lost
in addition to the £20,000 already spent. Cox was not a man to
accept defeat, but conditions were against him, and further
attempts to raise *Hindenburg* that year were abandoned, partly,
too, because the weather at that time of year was so uncertain.

8

Moltke's *Last Voyage*

ON THE DAY AFTER the temporary abandonment of the attempt to raise *Hindenburg*, undeterred by his costly failure, Cox climbed on to the bottom of the battleship *Moltke* which lay awash at low tide between RYSA Little and Cava. She was bottom-up in 78 feet of water and, of all ships in Scapa Flow, *Moltke* was the most dangerous to navigation. She was on a fairly level, but slightly soft, bottom, with a list of some 17 degrees.

Moltke was an enlarged version of *von der Tann* and had the same protection as a battleship. Five pairs of 11-inch guns were set in five turrets on the centre line of the ship. This turret arrangement also followed that of *Kaiser* class ships, but her low freeboard had caused her forecastle to be awash in anything like a heavy sea. Her crews had always looked upon her as being a lucky ship.

Of the £100,000 with which Cox had begun operations, only £10,000 now remained, but *Moltke* would be worth a considerable sum as scrap. A surveying crew had reported that her bottom valves and other openings could be sealed from the outside. Still attached to her was a large boat made of two-ply oak in wonderfully good condition. The boat was detached, floated and towed ashore in good shape. Water inside *Moltke*'s hull could be driven out by pumping in compressed air after sealing apertures. The deck openings would be convenient vents through which expanding air could be released as she surfaced.

Petersen, Cox's chief diver, reported that there was ample room to blast away funnels, the crashed foremast and all other hindrances which might prevent the ship from floating. In this, as in several other ships, the gearing for the operation of the armoured doors weighing several tons had been sabotaged, giving the salvage crews much additional work. Twelve inches of solid steel in the centre sections tapering off to about four inches fore and aft, provided the main side armour, and 12-inch armour encircled the main conning tower. Seaweed and other marine growths on the bottom and hull were as high as a diver's head and so thick that they could be removed only with knives and axes, some of the stems being as thick as a man's wrist. This growth had to be cleared away before bottom valves could be located.

After careful consideration of all possibilities, Cox decided to use compressed air. There was nothing new in this. Compressed air had been used in 1909 to raise SS *Fleswick* which sank after a collision in Cork harbour. In 1925 Captain John Iron used it to raise the monitor *Glatton* which had rested upside down since 1918 in Dover harbour. General Ferranti and Major Gianelli had used compressed air to float *Leonardo da Vinci*, a 24,000-ton Italian battleship carrying 13 12-inch guns which had been blown up and sunk in Taranto harbour on the night of 2 August 1916 by an enemy bomb, secretly introduced into one of her magazines. She had come to rest in 36 feet of water, and her gun turrets and funnels, resting on the bottom, had been forced into her hull until the upper deck was buried. When she had sunk 30 feet into the mud, her funnels had reached a bed of clay which had arrested further sinking.

Yet, though the general principles of using compressed air had been established, the method was new to Cox. Moreover each ship presented its own particular problems. Cox had read an account of the Taranto operation, and he was further assisted by Major Gianelli who visited Scapa Flow to see his work there and exchange information with him on their respective methods of approach to salvage tasks. One major difference between the situations of the Italian ship and *Moltke* was that while the former lay in a sheltered position with a list of only eight degrees, *Moltke*'s list was 17 degrees and she lay upside

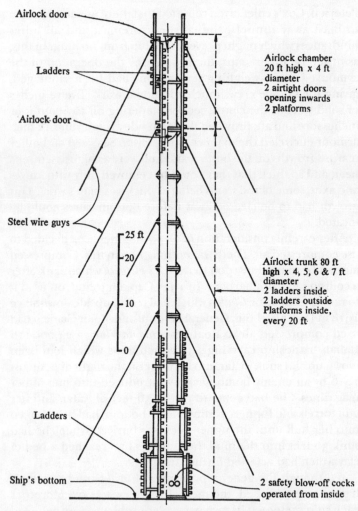

Airlock door

Ladders

Airlock door

Airlock chamber
20 ft high x 4 ft
diameter
2 airtight doors
opening inwards
2 platforms

Steel wire guys

25 ft
20
10
0

Airlock trunk 80 ft
high x 4, 5, 6 & 7 ft
diameter
2 ladders inside
2 ladders outside
Platforms inside,
every 20 ft

Ladders

Ship's bottom

2 safety blow-off cocks
operated from inside

Figure 2. General arrangement of 100-foot airlock.

down in water often whipped to a fury by storms. A ship with
the lesser degree of list would right herself when raised by
compressed air, but one with a much greater list could not do
so.

After a week of bleak, wintry weather and October gales which
stopped all work, concrete was used to block the bottom valves

and lower torpedo tubes. Connections for air-pipes were made along the hull, and the compressors were run night and day. To lighten the ship's weight, the giant propeller was loosened, worked off the shaft and hoisted out. Ten days from the commencement of pumping in air, the fore end broke surface, but the stem was still down. She also developed an alarming list, and when it was found that she was not watertight she was allowed to settle again to the bottom.

Divers now had to work in compressed air inside the ship to seal the transverse bulkheads and thus divide the ship into watertight compartments. No drawings of the ship were available, so there was no alternative to piercing the hull and fixing an airlock on that part of the bottom exposed at low tide. The divers commented that under the grey, northern sky and its bitingly cold winds, working under the water was the best place and they were comparatively comfortable. Up above, seas frequently washed over the boat from which operations were conducted.

An air-lock is an airtight, steel-plated chamber employed to prevent the escape of compressed air while men enter the hull to work in the space created by air-pressure above the level of the water. A hatch, or door, at each exit from the lock permits the safe entrance of men and materials, one hatch being opened while the other leading to the high-pressure area is shut. When the open-air hatch is shut, a man opens a valve which admits high-pressure air to the lock, and when the pressure is the same as that in the hull, he can open the lower hatch and descend into the hull. When he climbs out, the procedure is reversed. A man's first entry into an air-lock could be a terrifying experience, for when the valve in it was turned there was a sound as though every engine in the world was letting off steam, while compressed air gushing in from the ship's interior thickened the air like an old-time London fog, and one's ear-drums seemed to be about to burst.

As Cox had not used compressed air, he had no experience of air-locks either, although they had been in use for 70 years or so.

The position for each air-lock was marked by divers on the ship's bottom. Angle plates were then fixed round the place marked on the low side so as to be able to locate the air-lock accurately when the time came to fit it. Meanwhile other divers attached eyeplates to take the steadying guys.

The first air-lock made by Cox was crude but satisfactory, then others were constructed. The tubes were made from disused steel boilers six feet in diameter and 12 feet in height. They were built in sections but taken out to the wreck in one piece in order to reduce diving work in deep water to a minimum. Steel ladders were fixed to them inside and out. Then the lock was positioned, bolted down and tightly sealed. Great care had to be taken in placing the air-locks to avoid frames and stiffeners in the ship's hull. Within this diameter of six feet, a man had to use an oxy-acetylene burner to cut an opening in the ship's bottom. As it was possible that problems would be encountered, McKenzie went down in the lock with the first man to begin cutting. The experience was unpleasant, for when the vessel had turned over, fuel oil and liquid in the bilges had poured over everything, and the intense heat caused foul, choking fumes to rush into the air-lock from the ship's burnt red lead, oil, paint and bilge-water. The two men hastily scrambled out and soon recovered in the fresh air.

The first air-lock was fixed in the forward boiler room near the forward bulkhead. After a second lock was fitted, men could work inside the hull without discomfort from bad weather whilst the ship was without buoyancy on the sea bottom. Hundreds of small leaks had to be sealed in the hull. Compressed air in the compartment helped to hold in place anything put in a hole, so sealing was easier than was the case with *Hindenburg*. Work was discontinued if violent weather prevented the men from passing between ship and shore. Even under the best conditions the difficulties were immense of fitting a tall air-lock swinging from a crane to a steeply-sloping keel under water in a current.

Inside the hull divers found an indescribable tangle of machinery, piping and everything which had fallen loose when *Moltke* had turned turtle. Much of the metal was corroded, and everything was plastered thickly with mud mixed with coal-dust and oil. The divers had submersible electric lamps and telephones, but there was always the risk of short circuits, apart from the constant danger of air-pipes being cut by jagged metal.

For safety they worked in pairs. Working conditions were often appalling but at last, by teams working above and below the water-line, they had three watertight compartments inside the ship – at bow, stern and amidships. Manholes were then cut through the bulkheads separating the various compartments, and electric cables run through them so that lights could be installed to work by.

McKenzie described the vast amount of work which had to be done before a ship was ready for lifting: all pipes between half an inch and 18 inches in diameter had to be cut through on both sides of the bulkhead and plugged with specially made soft wood plugs. The plugs, set in red lead putty were driven home, and if over three inches in diameter shored to a convenient point. Cement patches for all compartments, which were as large as 20 feet by 16 feet, for boiler rooms etc, were held in place by shutters and toggle bars and the edges sealed with oakum or tallow. The rubber sealing strips had perished on many watertight doors, and the doors themselves had buckled badly under the rush of water as the ships capsized. These doors had to be forced open and relined with oakum, felt or spunyarn soaked in red lead. Sills had to be cleaned and dressed up with a file to remove high spots, and the doors then closed and strongbacked. Badly buckled doors had to be removed, and the resulting apertures shuttered and concreted, or fitted and caulked with stout wooden patches faced with pudding joints. These, too, had to be built. Then stages had to be fitted in stokeholds and bunker spaces to provide access to doors which had to be closed, the ships being upside down, of course, and the doors up to 20 feet *above* the nearest deck. The many compartments could not be reached by the normal means of access, so it became necessary to drill through armour plate up to three inches thick and through hundreds of panels, and to fit new ladders before the work of reclamation could proceed. When all the transverse bulkheads had been sealed effectively, the longitudinal armour bulkhead forming the bunker wall on each side had to be treated similarly, so that control could be exercised over the list of the ship before it could be raised. After bulkheads had been sealed to a low level, great care had to be taken in case the ship rose prematurely; not more than two compartments were allowed to be pressed down at any one time, other compartments were exhausted and the water level was allowed to rise to maintain negative buoyancy. A.S. Thomson, who had watched the scuttling of the fleet from the top of a hill near Lyness, was in charge of this part of the work. In recalling these days, he said that no special working clothing was worn, and that the worst part of the work was when one emerged from the top of an air-lock in wintry weather and had to descend the pitching lock in biting wind.

McKenzie was in charge of the team scaling the side-tanks inside the ship. There was a scare when air began to vaporise, an indication that pressure was being released and that water would rise inside the hull. McKenzie immediately ordered a stoppage of work and instructed the men to get out. To do so, some had to climb back through four manholes in the bulkheads, feeling their way in darkness as the lights failed, until they reached the air-lock entrance with the escaping air at gale force blowing their jackets over their heads. But it proved to be only air rushing into the forward end of the ship which was rising, the cause being the closing of a valve by a man who had misunderstood an order.

By May 1927 the ship was watertight and all sections could be inflated independently or together. It was a noisy, animated scene with the throb of compressors on the tug, and *Moltke* surrounded with rubber pipes of all descriptions which squirmed in the movement of the water like monstrous sea-snakes, while a maze of electric cables supplied the plant installed inside her. Before the lift took place, the main sections were charged to bring the ship within about 1,000 tons of the established figure for positive buoyancy. Pressure was first applied to the low side bunkers until the list began to decrease, and then to the high side bunker space until pressures on opposite sides were equal just before the inclinometers registered zero. Pressure was then increased in all sections as required. Lifts were invariably timed to take place at lower water. Maximum advantage was thus obtained from the lower head of water outside the ship, and therefore there was a greater displacement of water inside.

But whether *Moltke* rose by bow or stern she had a steep list.

A destroyer and a pontoon were therefore grappled to the starboard side and sunk to keep her down, and the two biggest docks were brought along the port side. The diving team then took down 20 nine-inch cables and shackled the ends to gun turrets. At low tide the cables were winched on the docks until they were taut. The combined force of the rising tide, mechanical lift and compressed air raised the ship, but not only was she still listing, but one of the nine-inch cables parted, followed by a series of explosive sounds as others broke loose in a chain reaction. The operation was stopped, *Moltke* was again lowered to the bottom, and divers went down to investigate. They reported that the cables, though taking the load, had been severed by the sharp edges of the deck. Metal pads were therefore made for them to pass over, new cables laid and a thorough cheek made of the hull inside and out.

All air-locks were fitted with specially tested pressure gauges with 14-inch dials, so that the pressure in each section could be read to the nearest quarter of a pound. Men equipped with lifebelts were posted at the top of each airlock to record the pressures on slates. The slates were held up, the figures on them read through binoculars by salvage officers on the tugs, and instructions shouted back through megaphones so that inlet and exhaust valves could be manipulated as required. The large exhaust valves on the top of each air-lock enabled pressures to be balanced and buoyancy to be kept negative until all was ready for the final lift.

As buoyancy increased in the forward section, and as the suction grip of the superstructure embedded in the mud was broken, there was a slight upward movement of about two feet a minute. Then the driving force of expanding air shot *Moltke* to the surface as a million and a half cubic feet of surplus air was expended in a few seconds, sending waterspouts soaring upwards. She still had a list, but it decreased to only two degrees as the hull climbed 20 feet above the water. The men on the airlocks had to hold on tightly until stability was obtained, and one of them commented ruefully, 'I don't know about lifebelts. It's flaming parachutes we want up here.'

A workman in a boat made fast the painter to the *Moltke* and was about to enter an air-lock as the ship rose. Feeling an upward movement, he glanced down and was surprised to see his little boat hanging down vertically by the painter. Tugs were quickly positioned and made fast, and the great chains anchoring *Moltke* to the docks were buoyed and cast off. During the nine months' work in *Moltke*, 30 men worked eight hours a day inside the ship with air pressures ranging from 15 to 22 pounds, and six divers worked six hours a day at a maximum pressure of 35 pounds.

When a ship was raised and secure, there was, of course, no further need for the great air-locks. They were therefore removed on the quayside and kept for use on other wrecks, small air-locks ten feet in height being fitted in their place for the tow.

Cox sought and obtained Admiralty permission to put *Moltke* upside down in their dock at Rosyth. (*Leonardo da Vinci* had been towed in this way, but only across Taranto harbour.) Then he had to find £8,000 insurance upon two-thirds of the ship's value and carry the remaining one-third himself. He had also to sign *Moltke* over to the Admiralty as security against any possible damage to the dock at Rosyth.

On 16 June the tow began to Lyness pier. While still between the two docks she suddenly stopped and the tow-line parted. Tugs failed to move her. Divers went down and found that one of the huge 11-inch guns had dropped forward with its muzzle thrust into the sea bed where it became more deeply embedded with every new effort to drag the ship forward. Next day the gun was blasted free. Six new lifting wires were passed under the hull and tightened up at low water, and as she rose with the next tide she floated seven feet higher than before and was beached successfully near Lyness pier with her upper surface 20 feet above low tide level.

Next morning Cox sent a gang to work on *Seydlitz*. Simultaneously machinery was removed from *Moltke* which was prepared for the tow to Rosyth. This part of the work, too, was also marked by ingenuity. *Moltke's* bottom, now high and dry in all tides, became a railway siding as the pier railway was taken up and relaid on the upturned hull. Six-foot square openings were cut over the engine and boiler rooms where the air-locks had been. A light engine towed a three-ton crane along the railway lines. Down below everything worth moving was cut up with oxy-acetylene burners into pieces which could be passed through the holes. The crane lifted out 3,000 tons of metal. Dock sections were moored alongside, and on them, ten-ton cranes with extending jibs swung the metal ashore. *Moltke*'s main components were: 1,700 tons of steel and wrought – and cast-iron scrap, 200 tons of armour and 312 tons of non-ferrous metals which included copper, brass, manganese bronze and gun-metal. The gun steel was valued for its high content of nickel and chromium which could be used with other material in the manufacture of alloy steels. For convenience in hauling, plates were cut to furnace sizes. Boiler plates and tubes were valuable as they were low in their content of phosphorus and sulphur, while the nuts and bolts used in securing the armour plate had a high nickel content.

finally *Moltke* was ready for her tow. The tow-rope of the leading tug was half a mile long except when quiet water was reached when it was shortened. A kitchen, bunkhouse and mess room for the crew were built on her broad bottom, and also a power-house with compressors able to maintain pressure inside the hull during the 200-mile tow through the Pentland firth and open waters of the North Sea to the Admiralty dry dock at Rosyth. Additional tugs were needed, but British and Dutch firms refused the job unless Cox would guarantee payment in case of failure. Finally, terms were agreed by the Towage, Freight & Salvage Co of Hamburg (*Bugsier, Reederei und Bergungs A.G.*) whose big ocean-going tugs *Seefalke*, *Simson* and *Pontos* arrived at Scapa Flow. The first attempt to tow out the hulk was a failure because the captains could not agree, but on Friday 18 May 1928 *Moltke*, upside-down, began her last voyage. The weather forecast was good when they left Lyness. Cantic was safely negotiated, and the tugs headed for Swona but were tested severely in their efforts to keep *Moltke* off the rocks. Sailing west they ran into bad weather which increased rapidly to a raging gale. It was impossible to turn back, and soon the tugs were being towed by *Moltke* in the opposite direction to which they were heading at full steam. *Moltke* wallowed in heavy seas which flooded the deck-houses built for the crew and the protective shelters for the compressors. Sometimes the rusty hull was completely out of sight, and in the deck-house, the water was knee-deep. As compressed air broke from the hull in gigantic bubbles she sank six feet, rolling with a list of 12 degrees on either side. They passed Snelsetter, Aith Hope and Torness and went into open sea. Then the tide slackened, the wind began to ease, and the tugs got *Moltke* moving again, so that the rolling diminished and the escape of air ceased. The sky began to clear, compressors restored lost buoyancy, and *Sidonia*, which had been brought alongside for her air-lines to be connected, was able to cast off. Before 08.00 hrs they had rounded Duncansby Head.

But they had escaped one danger only for another. Arrangements had been made for an Admiralty pilot to meet the tugs at Inchkeith. However, a Firth of Forth pilot was first on board, and when Cox arrived with the Admiralty pilot, the former pilot, who had been engaged by the German captain, refused to give way. Still arguing, the two pilots failed to notice that the Forth Bridge was looming up and that the tide, which had a five-knot run, had carried the tugs to one side of its central pier while *Moltke* was on the other. The tow rope caught on Inchgarvie island in the middle of the Forth, dragging gear off the stern of one of the tugs. One tug scraped the outlying rock, but fortunately no damage was done. Hastily the cable was cast off. Cox scarcely dared look, for if the centre bridge was struck by that tremendous weight, the cost of the resultant damage could ruin him. But upside-down, engineless and out of control, *Moltke* passed safely through the central bay, and tugs, one lashed on either side and one pulling, took her in tow again, and delivered her at Rosyth.

To be able to enter the dry dock at Rosyth, a vessel had to be canted 90 degrees in the inner basin from which it proceeded into one of three dry docks. The limiting factor for a ship's draught was the sill of the caisson (a gate) at the inner end of the entrance lock. This had a depth of some 40 feet at high water during ordinary spring tides. With the superstructure blasted off, hulks had seldom more than a foot to spare with a draught of 39 feet, but there was always the possibility that a stanchion, or some other part hanging loose after a rough passage from Scapa Flow, could damage the sill of the entrance lock. On one occasion the dockyard officials asserted that damage to the dock had been caused, and they insisted upon repairs being undertaken. The entrance lock had therefore to be pumped out. As the dockyard had no compression pumps available, the pumps aboard the salvage tugs had to be used, and the task took a fortnight. A monumental granite mason brought from Aberdeen found a small piece of granite about the size of a saucer chipped out of the groove in which the caisson sat. He dovetailed in a new piece which the Admiralty inspector found to be less than three-thousandths of an inch at variance with the original piece. To prevent such accidents in future, piano wires were strung across the entrance lock six inches and 12 inches higher than the inner sill but positioned several hundred feet in front of it. The wires were led up the side of the lock and fixed under high tension to a spring and pointer on a heavy spring balance. Any obstruction touching the wire was reflected by the movement of the pointer, while the distance of the wires from the sill gave time for the vessel to be stopped before any damage could be done, though to bring 25,000 tons to an immediate halt entailed the ship being warped into dock at snail's pace. If an obstruction was recorded, a diver went down to cut it away. As an additional precaution, one of the dock officials armed himself with an instrument like an outsize Alpine horn. One end rested on the piano wire, the other was at his ear. Before long he shouted excitedly for everything to be stopped. Much shouting followed as the warping wires brought the old battleship to a halt. Then followed a sheepish apology from a red-faced official who explained that a labourer in the docking party had been keeping time with his foot on the wire at the edge of the dock to a tune he was whistling, and the docking was allowed to continue. When she was safely docked, Cox flung his megaphone into the air, yelling with relief, and was then seen to double along the ship's keel from which he had been directing docking operations in order to hand each of the two divers a treasury note – a bet he had lost with them that the wreck would scrape the sill upon entry. The tug *Sidonian* had been in attendance for five strenuous hours during the docking, and now she cast off, her raucous siren blaring the news that *Moltke* was safely docked. Scores of worm-like tubes, the homes of marine animals, were stuck to *Moltke's* sides and she was all colours of the rainbow with barnacles and sponges, the blue of mussel shells and the varied colours-red, orange and blueish-yellow – of anemones. A large quantity of plates and glassware were brought out of her by the breakers, the Alloa Shipbreaking Co Ltd, but the most sinister find was a cat-o'-nine-tails with a short handle and a bunch of thongs.

9

The Big Ships

IT WAS NOT UNTIL January 1930 that another attempt was made to lift *Hindenburg*. During the first three months of the year the docks were fitted out, new machinery installed, the plant overhauled and many other matters given attention. Meanwhile much experience had been gained on other vessels. When divers thoroughly examined *Hindenburg* they reported that some 500 patches were still watertight. The other 300 were then either remade or repaired. One patch alone cost £500 as the work on it had to be done under water.

To improve the stability of the vessel, the massive forward gun turret, the tripod mast and the heavy superstructure were removed. Then, to prevent her from heeling over when the bow was raised, a great concrete wedge was made 40 feet long by 30 feet wide to go under the stern on the port side where she listed. This was made from the engine-room section of a destroyer, and it was towed out and filled with 600 tons of concrete at a total cost of £2,000.

Everything possible had been done by the end of June. Much of the superstructure, including gun turrets, had been cut away. To ensure that pumps were positioned properly, four circular steel cylinders, each seven feet in diameter and 20 feet in length, were fixed over the ship's hatches and securely bolted to the deck. Holes were drilled through the bottom flange of the cylinders and through the ship's deck. Divers working inside the ship then passed bolts through these holes, and they were screwed up by divers on the deck. When the cylinders had been caulked and made watertight, they had, in effect, produced four coffer-dams (watertight cases) through which submersible pumps could be lowered, and through which anything discharged by the pumps could be directed. These coffer-dams also provided easy access to the ship, or a means of escape from it when pumping began. Two forward pumping stations were under the fore bridge, and the bridge deck entrances themselves formed a coffer-dam and a means of entrance or escape.

When pumping began and *Hindenburg* rose, she was at first steady, but when the bow was 16 feet up she began to list and sink again. The pumps were kept going but, though the block on the port side prevented her from tilting that way, Cox ordered his salvage officer to build another block on the starboard side, then, disgusted, he turned his back on Scapa Flow and disappeared on a three weeks' holiday.

While he was away, divers discovered that the trouble was caused by the outlets of the pump discharge pipes being under water. Adjustments were made and a diver went down to check the work. In darkness, 30 feet down, his arm was sucked up to the shoulder in an eight-inch valve opening. At a cost of £400, water had to be let back into the ship to reduce the pressure outside, and the diver was released, suffering no more than slight shock from an experience which could have had serious consequences. Pumping was renewed, and on 23 July the ship rose and remained level, but the deck began to bend under the strain. The ship then rose higher and began to list slightly.

During the pumping, Cox had placed a man wearing a lifebelt on *Hindenburg*'s deck. He was in little danger as several boats were handy if the ship turned over. His task was to call out the angle of tilt which he obtained from a special scale on the bridge. By half a degree at a time the angle increased from two-and-a-half to six degrees, and it began to look as though yet again their labours were in vain. Suddenly the list stopped. After 15 minutes it increased to six and a quarter degrees, then it fell again to six and the danger was over.

The decks were still awash with trapped water, but Cox was

the first aboard to celebrate the raising of the biggest ship ever salved up to that time. It was reported that he had spent £30,000 on the task.

While water was being pumped out of the hull the deck was found to be bent by pressure, the stern had been crushed by the weight of water, and the divers' reports were terrifying, but Cox went down himself and decided that work could safely continue.

Next day *Hindenburg* was beached in Mill Bay. Mrs McKenzie, wife of the salvage officer, found the crow's nest of the ship a delightful place to occupy for her reading and knitting on a warm summer afternoon, but after the jib of a crane had swung dangerously against the mast, her husband forbade her any further use of this airy platform. (The German translation of this book points out that Hindenburg did not have a mast such as that described, and the incident mentioned by Mrs McKenzie must therefore refer to some other vessel.)

On 23 August, 11 years after *Hindenburg* had been scuttled, three tugs took her in tow. It almost seemed as though the fight had at last been knocked out of her, for three days later, after a 280-mile tow, she arrived at Rosyth in the Firth of Forth for breaking up after an uneventful voyage. It was interesting that, when Metal Industries Ltd broke her up, they came across a bronze, or possibly gun-metal crank case which presumably had been manufactured about the time Germany was extremely short of copper alloys.

Meanwhile work had continued in *Seydlitz*, a ship which had taken part in the bombardment of Scarborough. *Seydlitz* had had the reputation of being an excellent sea-going vessel. She had been fitted with special gear for rapid coaling, and had well-placed bunker hatches. At Jutland she had been hit more frequently than any other surviving capital ship and had, in fact, reached harbour with her forecastle awash. Basically, she was an enlarged version of *Moltke* with a higher freeboard. She lay on her beam ends in 12 fathoms, her port side 25 feet above water, so that strangers entering Scapa Flow sometimes mistook her for a small island. Cox's broad plans were to raise her as he had done *Moltke*. Even so, he ignored the advice of his salvage officers and decided to bring her up sideways. He began by removing from the port side above water level 1,800 tons of 12-inch thick armour plating in order to lower the centre of gravity. This left a flattish space on which he placed cranes, deck-house shelters and air compressor units, also eight air-locks, each six feet in diameter and six feet in height.

Because of his intention to raise the ship sideways, more openings had to be scaled than in *Moltke*, and some were much larger. *Ciment fondu* was used with reinforcements of wood and metal where necessary. One funnel opening measured 46 feet by 29 feet, and the patch was made of 12-inch timbers reinforced with steel girders. Patches for ventilators measured 30 feet by 15 feet. They were made airtight and strong enough to withstand both heavy storms and a pressure of 20 pounds to the square inch from within. During this time the wages bill was more than £1,000 a week.

By June 1928 eight airtight compartments had been made in the hull of *Seydlitz*, and each one could be pressurised separately. Despite the warnings and misgivings of his salvage officers, Cox felt confident that the battlecruiser could now be floated. All structures except the deck shelter were cleared from the ship, the compressors began to beat, and *Seydlitz* came up dead level and not sideways as Cox had originally anticipated. When success seemed assured, a muffled noise from the forepart of the ship was followed by a dull explosive concussion as a bulkhead collapsed due to a large patch giving way unexpectedly. This caused the nearest bulkhead to it to give way also, and one after another the remaining bulkheads collapsed. The position was ominous. Cox hurriedly ordered all men out of the ship. Screaming air from the wrecked compartments rushed to the bows and altered the centre of gravity. The bow end swamped small craft alongside with tons of green water as she reared higher and higher. Then she rolled 48 degrees until her keel showed. There were awful sounds of rending steel as almost upside down she tore bollards from the sides of the floating dock and sank in a mighty turbulence of water and spume, snapping cables and with her air-locks and other structures completely submerged. The disaster had been caused by the removal of the 1,800 tons of steel, which may have been Cox's way of raising funds for he had lost no time in shipping it to America, though other reasons for its removal had been advanced at the time. Now, due to his lack of foresight, his men had to toil on the shore at Lyness filling sacks with sand until they had replaced in *Seydlitz* a weight equal to that removed in order to secure stability during the tow to Rosyth.

When divers could go down again, they found the bridge, the remains of 'the mast and the superstructure all crushed by the immense weight above them. Expensive patches were ruined; air compressors and the diving units on the hull were submerged, and nine months' work and expense were wasted, for the hulk lay even deeper than before at an angle of 48 degrees. She had been stopped from turning over completely by two funnels and a mast which had been left in place. The work had to be begun all over again, and new and longer air-locks fitted to the ship's bottom which was now uppermost.

During the next four months divers cut away all upperworks from the ship, now 70 feet down, to prevent her from turning turtle completely. It was finally decided to lift her upside down like *Moltke*. There was thus no need for watertight compartments as before, for she could be pumped full of air and raised like an enormous tank. Her sides and bottom were checked to make sure they were airtight, and by early October the compressors were building up pressure again.

This time her list was slighter as she rose, but suddenly, for no apparent reason, she rolled and listed to 50 degrees, which was greater than before. Once again pressure was released, allowing *Seydlitz* to sink to the bottom. During the next month she was test-raised 40 times by bow and stern until they were sick of the sight of her, and every time she cleared the bottom she still had such a list as to be obviously unstable. All kinds of devices were tried unsuccessfully, including the lashing of a destroyer to her hull and filling it with water to provide a greater righting force. At last she was raised high enough for divers to be able to place some open-ended boilers under her low side, taken from scrap at Lyness. These were filled with quick-setting cement, and *Seydlitz* was gently lowered on to them until she was tilted to the required upside-down position, in itself a laborious and expensive task costing many thousands of pounds. She still had a list when test-lifts were made, but she was now stable. After she had been sunk yet again, the big floating dock was brought alongside, and *Seydlitz* was pinned to it by 22 nine-inch cables.

All Cox's associates agreed that he was a great and courageous salvage man, but like all men he had weaknesses, and one of them was a desire for public acclaim. *Seydlitz* was now almost ready for lifting. All the elaborate arrangements had been completed. Cox fixed the day, arranged for the presence of reporters from the national press and of camera crews from *Pathé* and *Movietone News*. He gave instructions that his time schedule was to be followed strictly and that he would be back on the great day after a short holiday in Switzerland. Then somebody blundered. On a very low tide too much air was pumped into the ship, and up she came in a perfect lift. Cox was notified in Switzerland. By telegram came his furious reply that *Seydlitz* was to be sunk again, and sunk she was so that Cox could be there prominently before the cameras on the appointed day.

On 1 November she rose inch by inch with no list, and she remained level. Then with a deafening series of explosions, ten lifting-cables parted, but the rest held, for *Seydlitz* was at last stable under her own buoyancy.

Within the hour the tugs *Sidonian*, *Ferrodanks* and *Lyness* were towing her to Lyness pier, only five miles distant, and there she was beached in eight fathoms. A railway was laid on her bottom, her heavy machinery cut out and her forward gun turret blasted off to reduce the weight, though this created a serious loss of stability. The long tow to Rosyth began on 29 May. Good weather reports had been received, but by midnight *Seydlitz* was rolling heavily in half a gale. Near the Martello Tower at Crockness, North Walls, the wire attaching her to the steering tug parted, and before she could be brought under control the turret grounded on the bottom and she stuck fast for three hours before she could be got off and towed to the Longhope entrance of Pentland Firth. In Longhope Bay she was aground again as a quantity of compressed air had been allowed to escape before her departure from Lyness. The last mishap was when the tow-rope of *Sidonia*, which was 150 fathoms long, swept overboard James Sutherland – one of the 11 hands building themselves a hut on the keel of their temporary home. Fortunately, Sutherland was rescued, none the worse for his ducking. The accidents proved a blessing, for Mowat, second coxswain of the Longhope lifeboat, who was pilot of the German tug, had time to examine the lead-line with which the Germans on the tug had been taking soundings, and he discovered that it was marked in metres and not in fathoms, to which he attributed the reason for having been led astray. After an angry argument with the German skipper he made a lead-line for himself and had no more trouble.

McKenzie, who occupied a shelter made from steel plate bolted to the hull, did not turn in at all that night. By daybreak *Seydlitz* was pitching and rolling badly in a gale-force cross-wind, and air was escaping. McKenzie ordered the tugs to turn her into the wind, and now great seas swept her from stem to stern carrying away a life-raft which broke the main pumping-line to the forward part of the ship. Metal barrels containing petrol and oil broke loose and careered along the hull until most of them were swept overboard. As the stern reared up, a box containing two tons of spares was torn adrift and flung against the steel plate deck-house which accommodated the crew. A gaping hole was torn in the steel plates, and through it poured heavy seas which scoured the hull. Fires in the stoves were doused and the stores in the galley were soaked.

At last the compressors were got to work again, though the tugs had to reduce speed by half. Instead of the normal three and a half to four days, it took seven days to reach the Admiralty dry dock. On the worst day they made only 17 miles in 24 hours, during which time they were swept by heavy seas for four consecutive hours. During one bad spell, McKenzie had only two hours' sleep in three days, then he put his head in a bucket of water to refresh himself and went on deck again.

At the same time work went ahead on the battleship *Kaiser* which diver Hunt and assistant diver Miller surveyed in 150 feet of water. All ships of the *Kaiser* class had been completed between 1912 and 1913, and they were the first German battleships with superimposed turrets and turbines. Several months previously work had begun on this 24,500-ton battleship, which at low tide lay only 20 feet below the surface. Work proceeded much as before; air-locks with ladders inside them were fixed, and stayed by guy-wires to the hull; bottom valves and other openings were plugged with cement; necessary patches were made and compressor units brought alongside.

Kaiser, too, had turned when she sank, though with a list of only eight degrees. Inside the hull divers worked in discomfort because oil fumes and the presence of coal dust, which was explosive when dry, debarred them from having any form of heating. The weather was too bad for dock sections to be moored nearby and when, cold and wet, the men came off their shift, there was no comfort to be had. Climbing up the air-lock in darkness, getting out of the hatch into a howling gale, and down the outside of the air-lock into a pitching pick-up boat caused many duckings and minor accidents. It was astonishing that no one was killed or even seriously injured.

As a precaution against the vessel listing further, the divers built two 30-ton concrete pillars on the sea bed to the lower edge of the armour plating on the low side, but this was not needed. The 200-ton turrets were blasted clear and when, on 30 March, the lift was made, it proved to be the easiest of all. It was a rule, rigidly enforced, that everyone should be off any wreck when it was lifted, but when *Kaiser* came up, A.S. Thomson emerged unexpectedly from a hatch with a bag of electric light bulbs; these were in short supply and he had remembered them at the last moment and gone back for them. Cox's outburst of wrath was softened by the lighthearted rejoinder that he had gone down to give her a push up.

The problem was soon solved of floating *Kaiser* past the obstruction of a concrete-filled boiler built some time previously on the sea bed but never used. The conning tower of the submerged ship was brought by tugs exactly over the boiler. Then the battleship was sunk until its whole weight rested on one point. The hull deck, which had been cut through by divers, collapsed, the conning tower section was forced up into the ship's hull, the compressors pumped air into her again and the obstruction was no longer a problem.

On the following morning *Kaiser* was towed to Lyness pier and gutted as *Seydlitz* had been. In perfect weather and without any untoward incident, she was then towed to Rosyth and delivered to the Alloa Shipbreaking Company.

There had, however, been a fatal accident to mar the success of the lift. Herbert Samson Hall, a diver of 20 years' experience who had been employed by Cox & Danks for the past five years, had gone below to close a watertight door. He was working in water only five feet six inches deep and had given the signal to come up. As he walked through the door he stumbled and fell and did not get up again. He was quickly brought to the surface where his face-plate was at once unscrewed and his suit cut off him. Blood was running from his ears and he was dying. Soon life was extinct. He was aged 45. Contrary to McKenzie's orders, Hall had gone down without his lifeline, though that might not have saved him. Two days later McKenzie went down to test the equipment. Under Cox's supervision he deliberately had the air compressor stopped and found that a good supply of air was still coming through after four and a half minutes, and that there was enough air in his dress for another two minutes. At the inquest it was found that Hall had died of asphyxia, and that this was possibly due to the weight upon his chest and compression of his lungs by the weight of his corselet and the weights upon his back. One of the divers who gave evidence said that he felt as light as a feather when upright, but that there would have been considerable pressure upon his lungs had he fallen like Hall. The coroner found that it was an accident that might have happened to anyone and there was no evidence of negligence.

Good luck as well as bad had attended the salvage of *Kaiser*, but luck of another sort was with *Bremse*, a mine-laying light cruiser. *Brummer*, one of the few ships not to be raised, and *Bremse* were the first fast cruisers to be designed for minelaying, and their mainmasts could be lowered to facilitate any attempts at disguise in case of necessity. At the time of scuttling, a British naval party had tried to beach *Bremse* on the south of Cava, and there she had turned over and sunk in 75 feet of water with her bow showing above the surface. She was perched precariously on a rock which fell away almost sheer, and it was feared that she might slip away. Now her bulkheads were sealed, and the hull divided into watertight compartments. The patching was done and an air-lock fitted. In the hull everything was covered with a film of oil, far more of it than had been found in any of the other ships. The three men using oxy-acetylene burners were accustomed to fumes and stench, but suddenly there was an explosion and the compartment was filled with flames. Blackened and shocked, but not seriously injured. the men got out safely. The fire was out when an examination was made, but during the two months of work there were constant small explosions of vaporised oil and several times they had to run to air-locks with flames pursuing them, but not a single man was hurt.

By the end of July all the superstructure had been blasted away. The ship was turned upside-down by the method employed in the case of the destroyers, and the compressors were brought into action. They were within measurable distance of lifting her when she toppled over on her side, and during the night shift she heeled over gradually and perched on the rocks close inshore. As she was unstable it took two days to raise her. Attracted by the barnacles and mussels on her, immense shoals of sillocks surrounded the cruiser. Thousands were killed by the oil and were left floating. Seagulls were attracted by them in tremendous numbers, as were seals which came close to the salvage boats. *Bremse*'s oil-fuel tanks were being cleaned out and the oil had been lit as the easiest way of getting rid of it; but the fire spread and, though it was brought under control, the wreck provided a striking spectacle with dense smoke pouring through the many holes on the port side and on the starboard side near the keel, and even through the joints of the steel plates. finally she was considered to be so unsafe that, instead of being towed to Rosyth, she was taken to Lyness on 30 November 1929 and broken up there.

On 10 December 1928, while work at Scapa Flow was proceeding, the White Star liner *Celtic* went ashore on Roche's Point while entering Queenstown harbour in Ireland. No lives were lost, but tugs failed to move her, and Cox lent some of his men from Scapa Flow in an attempt to refloat the wreck. Among them was Malcolm Carmichael, one of his most reliable divers. By 27 November 1930 the holes had been patched, and air was pumped in to test their efficiency. But grain in the cargo had fermented, giving off a gas which converted the water into a poisonous liquid, filling the engine room and saturating the hold as the result of a fracture in a suction pipe. A man entering the hold was overcome, fell off the ladder and died. Carmichael went down to rescue him and died also. This one operation cost the lives of two other men in addition to these two, and 16 others were gassed.

Before *Hindenburg* had left Scapa Flow, work had begun on the battlecruiser *von der Tann* which had been completed in 1910 in less than two years, the shortest time for any German capital ship. She was the first German battlecruiser and first large German ship to have turbines and quadruple screws, and she had much better protection than any contemporary British battlecruiser. Now she lay bottom up in 90 feet of water with a list of 17 degrees. At low tide, 24 feet of water came over her port side. In general, work was of the same pattern as on *Kaiser* but, as the weather deteriorated, it became too rough for the docks to be held alongside and the work was done from the tugs. Even so, several hours sometimes elapsed before tugs could get alongside to take off the workmen who had often to wait in cold and darkness most of the night.

Inside *von der Tann* the air was foul, and explosive gases arose from decaying matter in the hull. Small fires started by oxy-acetylene cutting were common until chemists provided a liquid spray which eliminated the risk of fire. For six weeks this work continued. Then the bow was raised to check the balance, to enable some bulkheads to be sealed and the ship to be blown out by expelling the air before she was lowered again. Some days later, three men – Sutherland, McKenzie (no relation to the salvage officer) and Keldie were in wading-suits working knee-deep in slush in a small cabin. It had not been sprayed with the chemical which had proved so effective elsewhere. McKenzie was descending a ladder, and had reached the bottom rung just as Keldie's flame-cutter sliced through a pipe. A violent explosion blew McKenzie back up the ladder with such force that he was knocked unconscious when his head struck the hatch-coaming. The slush rose rapidly in the shattered cabin, and McKenzie came round after gulping in water. Keldie said he thought McKenzie's back was broken. The cabin doorway was blocked and the water reached Sutherland's armpits. He helped the other two into the highest corner of the tilted cabin. They could hear men tapping on the deck above them, but had nothing with which to tap a reply. When water reached their shoulders escape seemed hopeless. But Thomson on the deck above saw a hose connection move. It led from the blocked door, and when he shook the hose, there was an answering jerk, evidence that someone was alive. If they used a flame-cutter to get through to the cabin it might cause an explosion, but there was no alternative. Luckily the gas in the cabin had been consumed. They found the three men high up in a corner with water lapping their chins, the trapped air having preserved them from suffocation. They were rushed to hospital where their burns and bad bruises were treated. Amazingly no one had been seriously hurt and even McKenzie, whose head injury was the most dangerous of their wounds, was back at work again eight weeks later to learn that *von der Tann* had been beached on Cava on 5 February 1931. When the weather improved she was towed to Lyness.

Midshipman Martin Keith-Roach who climbed over her there, found several numbers of a temperance periodical in a watertight locker, still readable after 15 years. Many Orcadians still have salvaged objects in their homes: shaving-mugs, vases, ash-trays, plates, decanters, cups and saucers, even musical instruments and telescopes. It is not surprising that little of a personal nature found had any great value, for the maintenance crews had not expected to be aboard long and it is unlikely they would have taken anything precious into hostile territory under such conditions. One memento, however, prized by Mr McCrone, the then chairman of Metal Industries Ltd, the firm which continued lifting the battleships after Cox & Danks had ceased work in Scapa Flow, is an ornate silver-plated punchbowl. This was not in the ship, but was found alongside it by a diver. The assumption is that either it was taken by a German sailor who dropped it at the moment of abandoning ship, or that someone had dropped it during the salvage work – in what circumstances one can only guess. Several wads of notes in tight bundles were found in *Emden*'s safe; these were in excellent condition apart from the edges being discoloured by salt water. This money was, of course, at that time quite worthless because of the huge German post-war devaluation and the consequent changing of their currency. There were also some small coins, corroded after immersion. A gramophone record of Dame Nellie Melba was easily recognisable when played. A brass desk reading lamp, after rewiring and being fitted with a new bulb, is still in use, as is a pair of cut-class decanters with silver-plated tops from *König Albert's* wardroom. The inscription with the date 1913–16 was legible when found.

Several ships' bells were recovered. *König Albert's* hangs outside the 11th-century home of Mr McCrone; *Derfflinger's* ship's seal and bell and the bell of *Friedrich der Grosse* were returned as a goodwill gesture to Germany with considerable ceremony in the late 1960s at Metal Industries' premises, Faslane Port, when a German frigate serving with NATO forces, dressed overall, paid a special visit to receive it. But perhaps the most spectacular memento is the great red flag with its black German eagle which Mr McCrone intends to have passed down as a family heirloom. It was brought to the surface so tightly packed that the water had not penetrated its folds through the long years of submersion, and its condition is as good as when it was last flown. This flag, at least, was not worn in a gesture of defiance when its ship went down. It was displayed prominently at reunions on what at first was termed Surrender Day, but later changed to Trafalgar Day lest the former name should offend an old enemy. The participants in that first reunion diminish with each meeting, but once a year the flag still evokes memories in the minds of the survivors of the memorable surrender. An item salved of greater practical value was a diesel engine of several hundred horsepower. Although it had been many years under the sea, it needed little attention to make it serviceable. The main item which needed attention was the valve gear. After rewinding the electrical generator and giving the engine a general overhaul it became a prime mover in the oxygen-producing plant with which Metal Industries made its own electricity. For many years it continued to provide power, and it doubtless strengthened the company chairman's belief that German equipment and armour plating were better than the British and that the Germans put more thought into their designs.

10

Cox Bows Out

Cox's salvage operations at Scapa Flow were reaching
their end. He had lost several thousands of pounds on this
aspect of his firm's business, and he had probably persisted so
long with it because he was stubbornly determined at least to
break even and to be able to refute the prophets who had
foretold that he would make a loss and be unable to raise the
ships.

He now turned to *Prinzregent Luitpold*. The keel of this
splendid battleship had been laid in Germania Yard, Kiel, in
January 1911 and she had been completed in December 1913.
She had capsized when she sank, and lay upside-down in 105
feet of water with a list of 20 degrees and with 36 feet of water
over her keel.

Air-locks were therefore again necessary, and 14 in all were
placed in position. Men cut their way to the bottom of the ship
with oxy-acetylene burners. Each section of an air-lock was ten
feet high. The first section was bolted to the bottom of the ship
by divers, then another section bolted to that, and so on, until
finally it reached the surface forming a kind of 'chimney'
tapering from eight feet at the base to four feet at the surface.
The 'chimney' was then braced by so many wire stays that the
whole resembled a monstrous spider's web. The ship was divided
into sections to make it more controllable. Each section was
provided with an air-lock, and on the port side these were 60

feet high in order to be above the water level. The problems encountered were much the same as before.

Foul air soon belched from the air-lock, but no one was worried as orders had been given that no flame-cutters or naked lights of any kind were to be used in the hull until the ship had been blown out twice and the air tested. However, she had full bunkers of coal and the water inside the hull was like ink. When the flame-cutters were first used, the resulting smoke caused no concern, and though a few small fires started they were easily quenched. As soon as men were inside the ship, compressed air forced down the water, and it was possible to begin patching and stopping leaks as they appeared. When necessary, divers worked inside the ship. A new man at first found it an eerie and unpleasant experience to work by electric light on the bottom of a capsized vessel fathoms deep at a pressure which caused nose-bleeding, aching ear-drums and a sensation that one's head was swelling like a balloon. Smoke was still a problem. One diver said they became so accustomed to ignited gas, which resembled will-o'-the-wisps, that they were more amused than scared until a nasty explosion occurred. In one particularly bad section, men had to wear smoke-helmets.

On 27 May 1931 *Prinzregent Luitpold* was blown out again and the air retested. A gang of four men went down to complete the sealing of the bulkhead in the forward end of the torpedo flat. The air was clean and they were provided with electric light by a generator from a tug along-side. The first indication that there was anything wrong was a vibration and a heavy 'blow' in the water on the starboard side which suggested an escape of air. McKenzie and his chief assistant McAusland had just come up from another compartment when the explosion occurred. They went immediately to the air-lock and saw that the pressure had fallen by two and a half to three pounds per square inch. The four men in the forward end were suddenly plunged into darkness, a terrific explosion blew them off their feet and water swirled about them. A bulkhead had collapsed, thus releasing the air pressure so that the level of water automatically rose. Scores of rivets had been blown out of the side plates and the sea poured in. Fortunately, the men had pocket torches, but the air was thick with smoke and the water was soon more than five feet deep. Water was also pouring into the air-lock up which they had to struggle as best they could. Tait, a carpenter, did not get out. An emergency signal warned the rest of the men in the ship to leave as quickly as possible. Extra air-pipes and compression power were rushed into the section. Divers and volunteers went down. Hunt and Mowat were both badly burned and dazed. It was impossible to go more than a few paces inside the ship because of the dense volume of smoke, so the rescue party went up to fetch gear. When they returned, pressure had fallen from 25 to $20\frac{1}{4}$ pounds, indicating that water must have risen 11 feet in a section which had formerly been dry. Three hours later, when the rescue party went down for the third time, they found Tait's body in the middle of the explosion. He had been knocked unconscious and then drowned. His job had been simply to check the water level when the foul air was becoming exhausted through a hole, about seven-eighths of an inch in diameter, which he had drilled. Hunt had been blown six feet along a passage before falling into the torpedo room. In a way he was lucky, for had he been on the other side where the bulkhead closed in he would have been squeezed to death or locked in. Peterson, the diver who found Tait's body. had gone down to search for him without stopping to obtain a smoke helmet, knowing full well the risk he was taking. The cause of the explosion was never known with certainty. At the enquiry, a jury blamed a short circuit in the lighting system, but McKenzie suggested that it could equally have been caused either by spontaneous combustion or a lighted cigarette, though smoking was strictly forbidden.

Except for sections forward and aft, the airtightness of bulkheads was not made good below the armoured deck. When there was any danger of the ship becoming buoyant, certain sections were flooded, and Cox issued orders that all hands were to be out of the ship and its air-locks before the surfacing took place. On the morning of 11 June 1931 when the ship was raised, the wind freshened and rain began to fall in sheets. Cox suspended work so that it would not have to be continued later throughout the night in miserable weather. It was still grey and misty on the following morning when pumping began at 06.30 hrs. Soon after noon the bows began to lift, and row after row of rivets slowly appeared above the water, then barnacles and long festoons of seaweed. At about 12.40 hrs there was an uprush of water and air bubbles, the air-locks rose higher and higher and in a violent swirl of water the underside of the rusty bows broke surface. In ten minutes, 100 feet of the ship's bottom could be seen, red with rust and covered with streamers of kelp. The *Orcadian* reporter was impressed by the unconcerned air of the hands as they stood by waiting for the heavy after-end to show. He noticed that they were busy with odd jobs. Diver Peterson, who wanted a new knife for underwater work, chalked out the shape on the blade of an old, rusty, two-handed saw. Burner Sutherland burnt it out with an oxy-acetylene flame. Fitter Wilson fixed the blade into a much-used brass handle, and Peterson had the knife while he waited. During this time, also, a hole was stoved into the side of a row-boat, and it was repaired and made ready for further work. A replacement boiler was fitted in *Sidonia*. Hundreds of small jobs were completed.

Now that the ship was afloat, upside-down, divers working outside the ship blasted off in deep water the remains of the funnels. The turrets were in position and there was sufficient draught to dock the ship without removing them. But the conning tower was higher than the turrets and prevented docking, so the wreck was towed into shallower water where there was a rocky bottom, and partially sunk again until she was supported only by the conning tower, which was forced by the weight over her well up into the hull until the ship was resting on her turrets.

When the attempt would be made to float her again the conning tower would tend to drop, so it was decided to make it secure. Three direct access holes were cut through all the decks from the bottom of the ship to the conning tower. The top block of a six-fold three and a half-inch wire with 100 tons purchase was secured by a large toggle bar resting on a hole cut in the upturned bottom. To support the toggle bar, the double bottom below was filled with cement. To secure the lower block, a hole was burnt through the ten-inch armour on the outside wall of the conning tower to take the pin of a five and a half-inch shackle, frames and plating being burnt away as necessary.

Three such purchases were used and set up while the ship was still resting on her conning tower. The burning of a hole for the pin of the lower shackle had to be carried out under compressed air as the position was well below sea level.

The King's Harbour Master who visited the ship at Lyness stated in his report, 'The forward conning tower would have dropped out had there been sufficient depth, but the ship had to be let down over it again, and it was then slung with a large wire purchase. The forward conning tower was thus hanging on the ship like a pendulum.'

To provide fairleads for the towing, four ten-inch tubes were sunk right forward through the keel into the double bottoms which were then filled with cement, and the tubes themselves were filled with railway lines and cement poured in to strengthen them. About 50 feet abaft the fairleads, two large bollards were bolted to the bottom on either side, and two more were bolted on about 150 feet abaft these. Two two-ton hand-winches were secured abaft the bollards so that the wires could be handled as required.

Two huts were then built amidships on the upturned bottom. The foremost was a power-house containing two petrol-driven compressors, an electric dynamo to provide lighting, and an alternating current generator for the pumps supplying circulating water for the oil engines of the compressors. The other hut was fitted with wooden bunks to accommodate the 14 men taking passage on her. The crew had their photographs taken with their cook posing at the back in a clean white jacket and chef's tall hat. Two short masts were erected for signalling purposes and to carry an aerial, and on the side was a large tank eight feet in diameter and 15 feet in length to hold water for cooling the compressors and motors.

A permanent air-line ran fore and aft along the keel with connections to each section so that air could be supplied to any part at a moment's notice. As protection for the huts in bad weather, a breakwater of steel girders was built forward. Two boats and a raft, lashed to the upturned keel, completed the equipment. Oxy-acetylene burners and all tools likely to be required in an emergency were placed aboard.

The ship, towed to Lyness after being raised, lay alongside *von der Tann,* but for the tow to Rosyth three German tugs were used: *See Falke,* 4,000 horsepower, equipped with diesel engines and described by experts as 'a particularly imposing vessel', *See Teufel,* 1,500 horsepower, and *Parnass,* 700 horsepower.

After leaving Lyness pier, *See Falke* and *See Teufel* went ahead with 120 fathoms of tow out. *Parnass* was on the starboard side, and Cox's small boat *Ferrodanks* on the port side.

The hulk was an extremely difficult tow and she kept veering more than 45 degrees on either side of the course. Cantock Head was cleared with great difficulty, and only the power of *See Falke* saved her from being carried ashore by the spring tide on to the point there. When they were clear of the rip tides in Pentland Firth, the tow was veered for the sea passage and the tugs took up new stations: *See Falke* on the port bow, *See Teufel* on the starboard bow, with *Parnass* towing ahead of *See Teufel.*

For her tow, *See Falke* used 90 fathoms of 18-inch manila rope, 120 fathoms of six-inch wire and 45 fathoms of two-inch studded cable made fast to the hulk. *See Teufel*'s tow was similar, except that four and a half-inch wire was used. When this long tow was veered the hulk still sheered nearly as much as before, though she remained on each sheer for longer periods. They made headway at about two and a half knots.

Bad weather and fog delayed them on the journey. They reached the Forth Bridge at about 15.50 hrs on the afternoon of 11 May 1932, and arrived at the lock entrance to Rosyth dockyard 75 minutes later when *Prinzregent Luitpold* was placed in the lock at high water. She was then floating upwards with a freeboard of from 18 to 20 feet and was found to be remarkably airtight after her rough voyage. Then it was found she had to be lifted another 18 inches before she could pass over the inner sill to the basin and so into the dock. But the task of docking her was by no means over.

To allow the vessel to settle, four crushing blocks had to be built. These consisted of solid masses of timber with steel cover plates so disposed that when the hulk settled, four of the turrets would bear on them. Then divers had to build up blocks to support the ship throughout her length. This was a very long operation as in many places the blocks had to be built up to a height of 15 feet. There was an overpowering stench in dry dock from rotten weeds and dead fish out of the ship and there were always gulls swooping down for the mussels scraped off the hull.

This was the last ship of the German fleet raised by Cox, and she was the largest vessel ever salved at such a depth by the use of compressed air. An expert on the staff of *The Engineer* who inspected the ship on her safe arrival stated in his report, 'We were struck by the excellence of the teamwork which we believe has played, and will again, no small part in the success of these salvage operations.'

Cox's eight years' salvage work left him £10,000 out of pocket, though the scrap-metal side of his business had been extremely profitable. In all, he had lifted 26 destroyers, six battleships and a light cruiser. After he retired, he spent much of his time giving lectures on his work for the benefit of charitable institutions. But gradually his health and strength began to fail, though he was 76 when he died, in 1959.

Before long, Hitler gave orders that the German tugs were not to be used in the ignominious task of raising German ships for scrap, and they were withdrawn. Their place was taken by Dutch tugs, and Captain Vet, an experienced sailor of fine qualities, was the chief tugmaster.

11

Metal Industries Ltd Takes Over

THE FIRM WHICH TOOK over where Cox left off was Metal Industries Ltd who had been buying and breaking up ships raised by Cox & Danks. It may be wondered why they should have undertaken the lifting of even more difficult wrecks, knowing how costly the operations had been to Cox. But Robert W. McCrone, the company's managing director, was a man as determined and forceful as Cox, but far better equipped both mentally and technically, while both he and his chairman, Sir Donald Pollack, were excellent administrators, a field of industry which Cox had not cultivated particularly well, though he was always courageous, ingenious and willing to accept responsibility.

McCrone had little desire for personal publicity or public advancement, unlike Cox, of whom it was common knowledge that he had aspired to a knighthood. Robert McCrone was born in 1893 and was educated at Merchiston Castle School, Edinburgh, from which he passed on to the Royal Technical College, Glasgow. He had barely completed his articles of apprenticeship when World War I broke out. He was commissioned as an engineer in 400 Field Company, Royal Engineers, and served in France from 1915 until the end of the war, winning the Military Cross and gaining a mention in dispatches. After a period of attachment, with the rank of captain, to French Headquarters on the river Marne he was awarded the *Croix de Guerre*. After the war he worked for a time in Vickers Armstrong's design office and was occupied on work connected with the dismantling of obsolete ships of the British fleet. Then followed two years' work with the Granton Shipbuilding Co laying out yards etc. Before he was 30 years of age he had, therefore, acquired a sound practical and theoretical knowledge and was accustomed to handling men.

With two other men who had fought in World War I, he formed the Alloa Shipbreaking Company. One of his colleagues was Stephen Hardie, a chartered accountant, who later on became the first chairman of the Steel Board when the industry was nationalised. The other was Dr Donald Pollack, Surgeon Captain RNVR, who had Harley Street experience and later became Sir Donald Pollack. Pollack had valuable contacts with senior officials in the Admiralty as the result of his war service. These three men were known irreverently in the works as 'The Three Musketeers'. McCrone soon stamped his personality upon his employees and was credited with the ability to recognise immediately the only machine in a workshop which might be operating at less than 100 per cent efficiency.

For various reasons, mainly connected with the depth of water at Alloa, the firm moved to Charleston down the Firth of Forth and took over the Rosyth Shipbreaking Company which had premises in the naval dockyard at Rosyth. These premises and other facilities were greatly extended, and the lease of a dry dock was obtained from time to time from the Admiralty for the breaking up of capital ships raised by Cox & Danks.

Metal Industries Ltd was formed in 1923 with McCrone as managing director, and Pollack as chairman. In 1950 Pollack retired and McCrone was appointed chairman in his place, a position he held until his retirement from the company in 1955. He became a director of British Oxygen Ltd, a member of the South of Scotland Electricity Board, a member of Lloyd's, a governor of the Royal College of Science and Technology of which he was also an associate member, a BSc of Glasgow University, a member of the Institute of Civil Engineers and chairman of several other industrial concerns. Today he still serves on the board of various companies and occupies himself with a wide and remarkable variety of public and private interests.

Cox was unfortunate when the average price of scrap fell

heavily; the new company could obtain double his prices. McCrone soon realised that other factors had contributed to the poor financial results of Cox's salvage work. Much of his equipment was worn out and out-of-date, his salvage ships were no longer suitable; his air compression pumps were inadequate for their tasks; his labour force was not used to the best advantage because of the obsolescent equipment and uneconomic methods. The new firm acquired first Cox's interests and then his equipment, the main item of value being the floating dock. They also acquired his labour force, including that indispensable figure, McKenzie. Cox had employed some 200 men but, as the work went on, the new firm increased this force by 50 per cent.

At no time was there any difficulty in the recruitment of labour, especially in the hungry 1930s when elsewhere there was considerable unemployment. The wages were not particularly high by comparison with industrial rates generally, but the promise of long-term employment at elevenpence halfpenny an hour for a 48-hour week with free accommodation was attractive. In practice there were no fixed hours, and overtime was worked willingly whenever required. In addition, whenever work in a ship's compartment was completed at a cost less than the estimated cost, half the saving was paid as a bonus to the crew concerned. McKenzie, employed at a comparatively low salary for a man of his ability, also received a handsome bonus of £5,000 on each ship lifted. He raised the company's eyebrows when once he lifted two ships in the same year.

The work held attractions other than guaranteed employment: comradeship engendered by living and working together for long years; the fact that a man could see his job through from start to finish; the deep satisfaction when the bows of a sunken ship broke surface in a spectacular eruption of water, oil and expanding air. The successful end to a difficult task was there for a man to see, and his excitement was renewed with each succeeding lift. The ever-present dangers spiced the hours of long, hard work. Labour relations were excellent, and during the whole of the salvage operations there was only one strike for better conditions, and that lasted for precisely ten minutes. Although Metal Industries was the first firm in Great Britain to manufacture liquid oxygen, this gas was not used in the lifting or breaking up of the ships for which gaseous oxygen was used. This was delivered to the ships through pipes so that no transportation costs were involved.

The new firm began energetically. The works were completely reorganised. Oxygen had been a considerable expense to Cox. The new firm made its own, but produced it in liquid form. This was easier to transport, cheaper in price and more convenient in every way. For example, oxygen could now be piped direct as required to the ships, and Metal Industries' 100 blowpipes had all the gas they needed; their new oxy-acetylene burners were operated by only two men compared with the gang of 25 previously needed. Liquid oxygen was also sold to other firms, thus helping to reduce overhead charges. The sturdy *Ferrodanks* was found to have outlived her useful life and was scrapped. *Mary Cowie*, a drifter, and the white motor boat, *Doris*, were bought for taking men to and from work.

Pollack, too, was a shrewd business man. For example, he visited steel works in Germany, arranged sales of scrap metal which he had cut into blocks of a suitable size to suit their furnaces, and it was he who decided that the ships raised by Cox were bought only after they had been safely docked, thus leaving Cox to bear the expensive insurance on them during the long tow. He, too, had many interests, and among them he was a vice-principal of Edinburgh University.

It was widely said that where Cox had failed, Metal Industries could not hope to succeed, yet with their more modern methods and equipment, and with better administration, they were able to make an average profit of £50,000 per ship.

Bertha, later converted for use as a salvage vessel by the Grangemouth Dockyard Company, was bought from the Southern Railway. Four compressors capable of pumping 2,500 cubic feet per minute were installed in her. She was also fitted with dynamos, workshops and everything necessary for the heavy work ahead. Her sheer legs and cables could lift 25 tons.

Then McCrone visited the Admiralty and bought *Bayern* for £1,000. Subsequent ships cost the company £2,000 each. *Baden*, which had been beached in a sinking condition, and *Bayern* of the same class, had both been completed by Germany in 1916 and were the reply to England's *Queen Elizabeth* class. They were the first German battleships to carry 15-inch guns firing 1,653-pound shells. They also differed in some respects from the *König* class: for example, the central barbette was suppressed and the positions of the after boiler room and engine rooms were transposed. *Baden* had not originally been earmarked for surrender, but was substituted for *Mackensen* which, in fact, was never completed.

When work began on *Bayern* some trouble was encountered and a Glasgow naval architect, Dr Douglas, was called in for advice. Later, when work was put in hand on *Grosser Kurfürst*, the second ship, Metal Industries decided that they needed a permanent member on their staff with naval architectural experience, and they employed Mr J. Robertson who returned from Canada in 1933. As this side of the work did not occupy the major part of his time, he worked inside the ships while they were at the bottom of the sea. When McKenzie suggested that Robertson should learn how to dive, he found a ready pupil. Describing his first dive, Robertson said that he dressed in the diving-boat near *Grosser Kurfürst* which lay by Lyness pier and, in heavy boots and corselet, stumbled to the ladder at the bottom of which an experienced diver waited for him at the rope leading from the ladder to the bottom 40 feet below. The weights were put on, then the helmet. Air was turned on, the face plate secured, and he was in a world of his own, feeling somewhat apprehensive. However, confidence returned when, seeing the diver waiting for him, he left the ladder and swung on to the rope, after which he enjoyed every moment of this new experience. The water was clear and visibility good. He was taken under the ship where everything was in shadow. He had some difficulty in seeing as his air had purposely been left somewhat low so that he would not 'blow up' (too much air could lift a diver to the surface). Unexpectedly he found himself on a piece of rope left between the guns of 'A' turret and promptly fell off. He learned later that the other diver held him by the arm and, after blowing air into his own helmet, got them both safely to the bottom. Later, when he had learned how to walk about, he was taken out into Scapa Flow, though he never attained the skill of an experienced diver.

Robertson, like others, pays a high tribute to the skill and endurance of the divers who worked both as divers and as foremen inside the ships. Outside the ship they worked in depths up to 200 feet in standard diving suits. The usual procedure adopted was for a diving party to survey the next ship to be lifted while the previous one was being prepared for her tow to Rosyth. Having located the ship, after survey they marked off the sections. Then from prepared drawings they fixed the position of each air-lock and made arrangements for fastening the guys. When the first air-lock in position could be used, work inside the ship began with the diver now acting as foreman in charge of the pressure workers. For this work he wore long sea-boots and oilskins. Meanwhile other divers were fitting the remaining air-locks and securing them with guys.

If a 'blow', or leak, occurred in a compartment, the diver would have to don his diving gear again and go down into the ship to seal it. When the ship was lifted and taken further inshore, it was the divers again who had to cut away turrets, mast and parts of the superstructure with explosives before the wreck could be brought as near to Lyness pier as was desirable. They also had to accompany the 'runner' crew, as they were termed, who lived on the hulk during the tow to Rosyth where they shored and fitted the ship in dry dock ready for the breakers. First on the job at Scapa Flow, they were last off at Rosyth.

Like so many of the ships, *Bayern* lay bottom up in 20 fathoms of water. She had a list of nine degrees and it was decided that the only way to raise her was again by the use of compressed air. At ordinary spring tides, 65 feet of water surged over her forward and some 85 feet aft.

Seven air-locks were fitted to her bottom to give access to the hull. They were enormous towering cylinders 70 to 90 feet in height, tapering from the base which had a diameter of seven feet. The longest weighed 20 tons, which presented the divers with a difficult job. They were built in 10-foot sections with 'resting' platforms every 20 feet, and with ladders both inside and outside. After they had been tested at Lyness to withstand a pressure of 90 pounds per square inch, they were towed out to *Bayern* in one piece to minimise the diving work in deep water. The seven sections into which the ship was divided enabled trim and stability to be maintained.

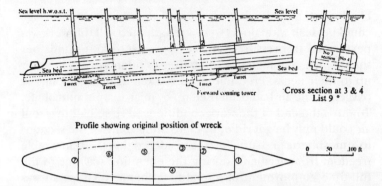

Profile showing original position of wreck

Figure 3. Bayern – *subdivision and position of airlocks.*

The divers had a tough time while the air-locks were being fixed. Two dozen cleats, or eye plates, had first to be bolted to the hull for guy fastenings. A circle of temporary holes was drilled accurately off a template, and all holes tapped and plate washers studded into them to take the bottom flange of the air-lock. As soon as it was lowered, two divers clamped down the lower flange with the plate washers. Meanwhile other divers passed up the ends of the wire guys to men on top of the air-lock. Working feverishly, these men made the wire guys bar-tight with stretching, or bottle, screws. These screws embody two spindles, one with a right-hand thread, the other with a left-hand thread. Both are in a common casing, and when the screw is rotated, it either tightens or slackens the attached guy as required. Then divers drilled permanent holes through the ship's bottom, using the lower flange as a template. When this work was completed – and it had to be done on all seven air-locks – water inside the air-locks and working chambers was expelled by air pressure. A manhole was then drilled through the hull and a similar hole through the tank top. Oxy-acetylene cutters could not be used because of combustible gases.

The seven sections, an air-lock to each, had then to be made watertight. A tremendous amount of work was involved in tightening bulkheads. Hundreds of pipes of various sizes were cut out and blanked. Ventilator casings from a few inches to several feet in size were cut away by hand, apertures in bulkheads blanked off and all kinds of valves dismantled so that leakage could be dealt with; doors were strengthened. All this work was performed in pressures ranging from 40 to 55 pounds per square inch, and men in wading dresses often worked in water up to their necks. Precautions were taken against foul air, for oxygen in the air had been used up by microscopic animal life. Towards the end of the work conditions were so bad that foul air could only be got rid of by exhausting some of the sections to atmospheric pressure. It was considered that the remarkable freedom from accidents during the operation was due to the full-time employment of a qualified chemist. This man was Cowan, a convivial soul, popular with everyone, especially at the parties which Metal Industries instituted to celebrate each successful lift. He was a member of the dance committee, and at the dances produced an overpowering concoction of his own which he named 'Nelson's blood'. The mention of Cowan's name is still enough to draw a smile from those who worked with him. Cowan took daily samples of the air in any compartment of the wreck where men were working, and tested them to ascertain if they contained traces of the highly explosive gas, methane, which was generated from rotting vegetable matter when air was pumped in. The equipment he took down could not have been simpler – a few penny balloons and a bicycle pump to inflate them partially. With these he entered the air-lock to take his decompression along with the shift coming out of the wreck. This would take between three-quarters and one and a half hours. As the air-lock pressure fell, the balloons expanded, and Cowan used to give the men a salutary lesson on the necessity for undergoing the full requisite compression period by explaining in picturesque language that what was happening to the balloons was happening in exactly the same way to their insides while they were being decompressed.

Cowan was 60 years old and was reputed to be remarkably astute. A story told to illustrate this was that once, for some reason, he was unable to collect a sample of air himself and asked a fireman to get it for him. The man did so, but somehow punctured the balloon on his way out of the air-lock. Rather than admit it, or go back for another sample, he blew into another balloon which he handed to Cowan. Soon after he had begun to analyse it, Cowan sent for the fireman and said, 'You'd better get something for your breath. It's foul'. Nothing, it was said, ever slipped his attention. He never minded going down to 50 pounds pressure to obtain his samples, and there was no case on record of foul air in a compartment which he did not discover in good time.

When a man works under pressure, air in his lungs, nose, mouth and ears is increased as the pressure rises. The air pressure must therefore be equalised on the ear-drums, and if the Eustachian tubes become blocked there is likely to be considerable pain, with bleeding at the nose and ears, and the ear-drums may suffer permanent damage. At high pressure the body tissues are rapidly saturated with nitrogen. After long exposure to high pressure, gradual decompression is essential if harmful effects are to be avoided, and the worker must be restored to normal atmospheric pressure without the liberation of nitrogen in dangerous quantities in his bloodstream and tissues. Decompression tables have been calculated giving the approximate periods for a man to stay in a decompression chamber so that nitrogen will safely leave his blood without expanding into bubbles so large that they cannot pass through the capillaries. The period of decompression varies with the length of time a worker has been in a condition of compression.

When a fresh compartment was opened Cowan was the first man to enter. It was his theory that the poisonous gas was thrown off by rotting tarpaulins. Once, when a man was reluctant to go down because of the risk of poison-gas, Cowan offered to prove

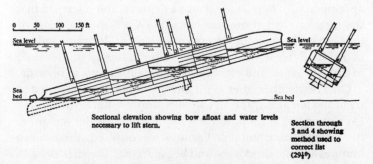

Sectional elevation showing bow afloat and water levels necessary to lift stern.

Section through 3 and 4 showing method used to correct list (29½°)

Figure 4. Bayern – *sectional elevation, bow afloat and $29^{1}/_{2}°$ list.*

that there was no danger of combustion by sitting inside the compartment and smoking a cigar.

On 18 July a main drainage pipe burst, allowing compressed air to rush into the forward part while the compressors were still busy. The wreck broke free and the bow rose prematurely 10 feet above water. The terrific expansion of air consequent upon this brought up the stern, and the ship rolled awhile as escaping air threw up great fountains of water. She narrowly missed surfacing upon the salvage ship, *Bertha*, which was moored close by. Then she lost buoyancy again and slowly sank. Divers discovered that when the ship had risen she had shed four gun-turrets weighing 2,500 tons. This had changed the centre of gravity, and much extra work had to be undertaken before another attempt at refloating could be made. For example, it was decided to crush the forward conning tower up into the ship. The conning tower was in two parts, comprising the heavily-armoured conning tower itself and a square armoured communication trunk inside the ship which extended through four decks. When the latter had been crushed far enough up into the ship, toggle bars were inserted into holes cut into it so as to hold the conning tower in the crushed position.

During this month, tragedy struck when John ('Busy') Bee of Portsmouth died on *Bertha* shortly after rising to the surface, having left the decompression chamber too soon. He was not a young man and the strain had been too much for his heart.

It had been intended to make the next attempt at lifting *Bayern* the following day, but weather conditions were unfavourable. Moreover, for no apparent reason *Bayern* had developed a list to port of about 42 degrees, and it seemed that she might roll right over on her side. When she had reached the bottom three air-locks were completely under water and out of action. Extensions were fitted to them, the list was reduced to three degrees, and for several days stability tests were made.

On 1 September, after eight months' work, it was decided to try lifting her again, and all compressors were put on full power. Every man was at his post when the 'stand by' order was given. five minutes later, 'cut pipe lashings' was ordered. Another two minutes and she shuddered and began to rise. The after air-locks had moved slightly as the stern freed itself. Every two feet of lift

Senior members of Metal Industries staff aboard *Bertha*. From left to right: T. McKenzie, the principal salvage officer, Commander Hughes, a naval architect, J. Robertson, naval architect and chartered engineer, C. Cowan, chemist and H.M. Taylor, assistant salvage officer. (*Associated Scottish Newspapers*)

Above A rare photograph of Messrs McCrone and Cox. (*Associated Scottish Newspapers*)

Below A work party, having completed their shift, have been taken aboard the salvage vessel *Bertha*. (*Associated Scottish Newspapers*)

Above A shift of pressure-workers leaving an air-lock. (*Associated Scottish Newspapers*)

Below A work party leaving a ship after completing their shift. They have had to climb up the inside of the airlocks and descend by the outside ladders. (*Associated Scottish Newspapers*)

Right J. Robertson, naval architect, inside a vessel on the sea-bed. This photograph was taken by flashlight as everything was in darkness. He is wearing wading-dress.
(*Associated Scottish Newspapers*)

Below Cowan, the chemist, aboard the salvage vessel, *Bertha*, with his air-testing equipment.
(*Associated Scottish Newspapers*)

Left Workmen in wading-dress inside a wreck under pressure on the sea-bed.
(*Associated Scottish Newspapers*)

Below Men entering *Bertha's* decompression chamber for treatment of caisson disease, or 'bubbles'.
(*Associated Scottish Newspapers*)

Above Divers working outside a wreck, S. McKenzie on the ladder and P. Taylor ready to go down. (*Associated Scottish Newspapers*)

Below *Bayern*, immediately after being raised. (*Shipbreaking Industries*)

Left *Bayern* passing under the Forth Bridge on her way to the breakers. (*Shipbreaking Industries*)

Below *Bayern* approaching Forth Bridge and under tow by three powerful Dutch tugs, *Zwarte Zee, Witte Zee* and *Ganges*. (*Shipbreaking Industries*)

Above *Bayern* being towed into dock at Rosyth on April 30 1935. (*Norval*)

Below Tugs towing *Bayern* up the Firth of Forth to Rosyth. (*Norval*)

Above The hut used for the accommodation of salvage crews on wrecks being towed to Rosyth. The central figure is Baker, a mechanic, who donned cook's clothing for the photograph. A. S. Thomson, referred to in this narrative, is seated extreme right. (*A. S. Thomson*)

Below Pressure workers entering the air-locks on *König Albert*. On the left, a diver is ascending. (*Illustrated London News*)

König Albert refloated. The salvage vessel, *Bertha*, is alongside. Wreckage dangling beneath the hulk must now be cleared away. The air-locks used were 100 feet high. (*Illustrated London News*)

Above *König Albert* with attendant tugs passing under the Forth Bridge on her way to the breakers at Rosyth. (*Star Photos*)

Below *König Albert* being berthed in No 2 dock at Rosyth. (*Planet News*)

Bayern's appearance some time after demolition began. (*Norval*)

The end of *Bayern*. (*Norval*)

Above Dutch tugs at Lyness preparing to tow *König Albert* to Rosyth. (*Associated Scottish Newspapers*)

Below The bow of *Friedrich der Grosse* breaking surface upside down amid turbulence of water and expanding air from inside the ship as pressure decreases. The men on top of the ten great air-locks experienced some dizzy moments until the ship became stable. (*Fox Photos*)

Above After quick adjustments have been made to pressures inside the ship, the stern of *Friedrich der Grosse* next breaks surface. (*Associated Scottish Newspapers*)

Below The huge triple screws of *Friedrich der Grosse* appear above the water. (*Fox Photos*)

Above *Friedrich der Grosse* safely afloat. The complexity of the divers' work is evident by the cobweb of weed-covered guys supporting the air-locks. To the left of the wreck is one of the pontoons and its crane which have been in use throughout the operation. (*Associated Scottish Newspapers*)

Below *Friedrich der Grosse*, securely afloat upside down with attendant salvage tugs ready to tow her to Rosyth. The hut on her keel is for the accommodation of the caretaker crew during the tow. The tall air-locks have been replaced by short ones. (*Associated Scottish Newspapers*)

Above The gun turret of *König Albert*. The ship, like all others except *Hindenburg*, is upside down supported by nests of blocks. (*Norval*)

Below These eight air-locks, 90 feet high, were fixed by divers to *Kaiserin*, and the ship is now ready to be raised. (*Illustrated London News*)

The bow of *König Albert* when the ship was in dock at Rosyth. (*Norval*)

Kaiserin successfully raised, her eight air-locks secured by a web of guy wires.
(*Fox Photos*)

Above *Friedrich der Grosse* in dock at Rosyth having one of her armour plates removed. (*Norval*)

Right Cutting armour from *Prinzregent Luitpold*. (*Shipbreaking Industries*)

Below *Friedrich der Grosse* seen from the bottom of the dock in an advanced state of demolition. (*Norval*)

Removing an air-lock from *Derfflinger* before her tow to the shipbreakers' yard. But World War 2 broke out and seven years elapsed before this took place.
(*Conway Picture Library*)

Above At work on one of the four giant screws of *Derfflinger*, each of which will yield some 36 tons of non-ferrous metal. (*Conway Picture Library*)

Below An air-worker in *Derfflinger's* cellar which is, of course, upside down. The bottles are empty as the high pressure which raised the ships also blew in the corks. (*Conway Picture Library*)

Above *Derfflinger* on tow to Faslane Port (at top of picture) in the River Clyde. (*J. Robertson*)

Below *Derfflinger* in floating dock at Falsane Port in the River Clyde. Breaking-up is well advanced, and the method of blocking up the hull to keep the ship upright can be clearly seen. (*J. Robertson*)

Commodore T. McKenzie, CB, CBE, RNVR, the principal salvage officer both for Cox & Danks and for Metal Industries Ltd. (*Mrs McKenzie*)

lowered the sea water pressure by one pound per square inch. The expanding air inside reached explosive force and *Bayern* shot to the surface within 30 seconds, the released surplus air projecting huge columns of air and water 150 feet into the air. So rapid was the rate of lift that even when the ship was ten feet above the surface, water six feet deep was still cascading off the bottom, the salvage steamers rolling heavily in the turbulence. Two million cubic feet of surplus air had to be expelled if the ship was not to burst with 50 pounds pressure per square inch at the bottom of the hulk and ten pounds at the top. Columns of water shot up as the air rushed out, and in 40 seconds or so the men on the air-locks were from 40 to 70 feet aloft swinging about until the ship levelled off.

The biggest ship ever raised from that depth of water was now ready for the breakers.

McKenzie considered this to be the finest piece of salvage the firm had undertaken, hampered as they had been by a bad summer, high winds and appalling weather.

On 2 September, 24 hours after being raised, *Bayern* was towed four miles and beached in shallow water about one mile from the base at Lyness. A few days later she was towed on a spring tide to Lyness where she was prepared for her 260-mile tow to the breakers' yard at Rosyth.

The next two ships to be considered were *König Albert* and *Kaiserin*. Both lay in deeper water, and *König Albert* was chosen as the first of the two. Her keel had been laid at the Schichau Yard, Danzig, in July 1910 and she had been completed in 1913. The *König* class of ships were the first German battleships with all turrets on the centre line. Their greater beam gave them good underwater protection, far better than any British battleships enjoyed. *König Albert* had missed the battle of Jutland, being in dock for a re-fit at the time.

In October 1934 four of the firm's best divers made a thorough survey of the wreck. They found her bow in 23 fathoms and her stern in 21 fathoms. She had a port list of about nine degrees, and was upside down with all her turrets and superstructure completely buried in soft mud. It was realised that salvage would be extremely difficult and that the only method of raising her was again by the use of compressed air. However, the salvage team now had plenty of experience, and their first task was to locate and seal with a rapid hardening cement all bottom valves, main inlets, submerged torpedo tubes etc. The ship was divided into six sections, and air-locks were made ashore in sections and towed out as was customary. As the lowest depth over the wreck's bottom was 85 feet, the air-locks had to be 100 feet long. These were the longest air-locks so far made, and the placing of these 25-ton cylinders in choppy seas as they swung from a 70-foot jib on the pontoon was correspondingly difficult. Fairly calm days had to be chosen for the work, in winter, at Scapa Flow, such days were rare. The first air-lock was fixed on 29 November. By the end of April 1935 eight air-locks were in position, and work inside the ship was being undertaken by some 40 men working in relays at pressures ranging from 45 to 55 pounds per square inch.

There were months of difficult and dangerous work spent in repairing the damage inflicted by the German officers and crew before the vessel was scuttled, and the far greater damage caused by the tremendous rush of water against bulkheads as she turned over. Again doors had to be strongbacked, heavy pipes broken and blanked, hundreds of cables, ventilators etc cut, and all apertures sealed before bulkheads could be made watertight. Frequent delays resulted from gales and other adverse weather conditions when transit between the air-locks and the salvage steamers was difficult and often dangerous. Sometimes workers on airlocks were surprised by sudden storms and were marooned for hours before the salvage steamers could take them off. There were also frequent illnesses from working in compressed air, though immediate treatment was always available on the salvage steamers and ashore.

By the third week of July 1935 all bulkheads were sealed and final preparations for the lift began. It was decided to make no effort to correct the list of nine degrees before the actual lift took place; the best and safest method would be to raise the fore end first, then correct the list if necessary, and finally lift the stern. On 27 July the forward sections were almost at lifting pressures when a south-easterly gale temporarily halted preparations. The new salvage steamer, *Metinda*, had to slip her moorings and anchor off to prevent damage. *Bertha*, however, was able to hold on and maintain air pressure in the wreck.

It was 48 hours before the gale blew itself out and *Metinda* could regain her position and resume pumping. On the following day *König Albert*'s bow began to tear free. It was calculated that some 3,500 to 4,000 tons extra buoyancy were needed to break the suction and to drag turrets, superstructure, etc, out of the mud. The surfacing dwarfed even the spectacular eruption of previous ships. For the first two or three feet the bow rose very slowly, then the terrific expansion of air carried the ship to the surface. The bow soared higher and higher until in half a minute it was 20 feet clear of the water, and tremendous spouts of air, water, oil and spray completely obscured the forward air-locks as a million cubic feet of surplus air escaped.

The port list increased slightly as the bow rose, but expanding air in the port bunker reduced the list to seven degrees, at which it settled. Everything now depended upon the quick and efficient execution of orders. No hitch occurred and in a few seconds 22 lines of flexible pipe and six anchor wires were smartly slackened or tightened on words of command. Compressors were connected two hours after the bow had lifted and in three sections pressure was raised almost to lifting pressure. Work continued until 22.00 hrs when operations were suspended until early next morning. Then compressors with a capacity of over 3,000 cubic feet of air per minute were connected aft. Just before 10.00 hrs the 'stand by!' signal was given. A few minutes later the stern freed itself and rushed to the surface; the salvage vessels rolled and sheered in the turbulence, but all wires held and the list disappeared. By noon there was a freeboard fore and aft of 14 feet, and the 100-foot air-locks stood like the chimneys of brickworks against the skyline.

On the following day she was towed two miles to shallower water and beached, her funnels, bridge and superstructure touching the bottom. Later these projections were blasted away, and the ship was towed to her doom at Rosyth.

One of the many tasks of R.R. Drysdale, manager at Charleston and Rosyth of the yards of Shipbreaking Industries Ltd, a subsidiary undertaking of Metal Industries, was the preparation of estimates of the sales value of scrap obtainable from each ship. The weight of the ship was calculated from the

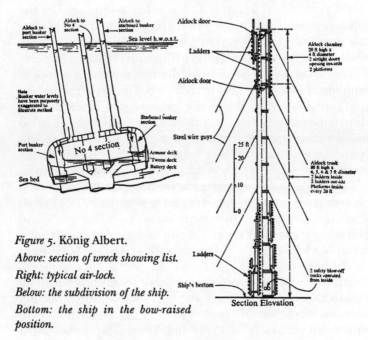

Figure 5. König Albert.
Above: section of wreck showing list.
Right: typical air-lock.
Below: the subdivision of the ship.
Bottom: the ship in the bow-raised position.

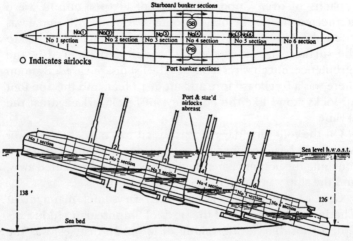

dimensions given in *Jane's Fighting Ships*. The weight of scrap was based on expected arisings from the original complete ship as no records were available to show if any tonnage was missing at the time of purchase. The estimated weight of *Bayern*, for example, less various allowances for water in boilers and a safety margin of ten per cent for losses from unforeseen factors and causes, was 23,520 tons. The actual out-turn based on the distribution of the ship's weight amounted to 22,012 tons. When the ship was broken up, the metal obtained totalled 20,835 tons. Its sales value was estimated to be £118,463 and, in fact, after a deduction for the cost of carriage, £112,784 was received, of which some £50,000 was profit.

Hindenburg, bought by Metal Industries Ltd from Cox & Danks, yielded 21,557 tons of metal, the greatest quantity. The smallest quantity, 16,172 tons, was obtained from *Moltke*. From five ships, *Bayern*, *König Albert*, *Kaiserin*, *Friedrich der Grosse* and *Grosser Kurfürst*, 99,439 tons of metal were obtained, consisting of 95,598 tons of ferrous metal and 3,841 tons of non-ferrous metal. This realised £629,670, a figure which represented a difference of only 3.9 per cent on Drysdale's estimates. It was this kind of meticulous attention to detail in all McCrone's overall administration of the operations which enabled Metal Industries to make a good profit where Cox & Danks had failed. For the curious, the residual remains of *Friedrich der Grosse* as shown by Drysdale's working papers are given in Appendix 3. The degree of accuracy in estimating the sales value is remarkable.

During this time armour from the salvaged ships was being bought by world markets. Considerable quantities were sold to Essen for Germany's new fleet, ironically at a time when England's own naval reconstruction was handicapped by the lack of top-grade armour plate similar to that being exported to Germany. Then Hitler's government began to make enquiries about the big guns, claiming that they were needed for coastal defence. As it was suspected, however, that the guns were wanted for second line vessels such as monitors, the British Admiralty was consulted about export licences. One morning a signal arrived from the Admiralty that the big guns were not to be exported, upon which the works manager rushed over to the dry dock and ordered the foreman to mutilate immediately the gun barrels and breech blocks of all big guns, and just in case the Admiralty extended its veto, to mutilate the secondary armament also.

Various methods were adopted for breaking up the metal, one at least, such as the 'dropping ball', having been in use for three-quarters of a century. This was used mainly on cast iron. A heavy ball on a wire jib was hauled to the maximum height by steam power. At the top it depressed a trigger which declutched a winch barrel and allowed the ball to crash down on the metal placed beneath it. Big electric motors were used to cut plates of hard steel up to two inches in thickness, and plates up to eight feet in length and one inch thick were within the power of large shears. Steel plates were detached from the hull entire and swung into the yard to be cut into convenient pieces. Twelve-inch plates could be cut at the rate of eight or ten feet per hour, and thin plates at 50 feet per hour. Between plating and hull of the capital ships lay teak three inches thick. Unfortunately there was then little demand for teak, but it was useful in the construction of McCrone's greenhouses, garden furniture and the doors of his house where it looks substantial enough to outlast time itself.

Soon after *König Albert* was docked Metal Industries received a signal from the Secretary to the Admiral of the Dockyard that her arrival had coincided with a large increase in the number of rats in HMS *Caledonia*, the boy artificers' training ship, and it requested that appropriate action be taken to destroy them. Metal Industries' manager promptly telephoned the secretary to enquire if his signal was to be taken seriously. 'It certainly is,' was the reply. 'Then', said the manager, 'our rats are easily recognisable. After fifteen years under the sea, they all have webbed feet and many have German SMS *König Albert* cap ribbons round their necks.' The matter was promptly settled by the touch of humour. 'For heaven's sake, cancel the signal and shove it in the WPB.'

12

The Last of the Big Ones

THE NEXT SHIP TO be tackled, *Kaiserin*, was a battleship which had been completed and commissioned in 1913. Her precise location was not known, but she was found within an hour by sweeping. She lay in 23 fathoms about three-quarters of a mile from the island of Cava, and three and a half miles from Metal Industries' base at Lyness. Divers fixed mark buoys forward and aft. *Bertha* was moored in position over her, and the company's best divers carried out a survey. They reported that the ship lay bottom up with a starboard list of 11 degrees. The water at her fore end was 23 ½ fathoms and aft 21 fathoms. Her superstructure and funnels were crushed badly as was expected, but the hull was sound. She belonged to the same class as *König Albert* and therefore all details of her construction were known.

The same method of lift as before was adopted, and air-locks were of approximately the same length also; the time for fixing an air-lock varied from one to several hours, weather being the main difficulty, as a 25-ton air-lock swinging from a 100-foot jib became a lethal weapon in the slightest movement caused by sea or swell. More than once, when sudden gales sprang up, the salvage team had to shelter on the pontoon before an air-lock could be secured. The first was fixed in July 1935 and the others at intervals of about two weeks. All were in place and secure before the end of October.

Yet again a highly dangerous mixture of combustible gases in the ship ruled out the use of oxy-acetylene or oxy-hydrogen cutters, apart from the fact that there was only 1.1 per cent of oxygen present. Constant analyses were made by Cowan. However, each section was exhausted to atmospheric pressure and recharged several times with fresh air, and the men could then work without undue discomfort.

Shifts could work for only short periods which varied daily from one and a half to three and a half hours followed by long hours of decompression under cramped conditions in the air-locks. To add to the usual difficulties of making bulkheads airtight and working in mud, oil and slime, bulkheads had been badly distorted by the rush of water when the ship had sunk and turned over while doing so 17 years before.

After testing and final preparations, everything was ready for the lift on 11 May. At 11.30 hrs the bow began to lift and it continued to do so very slowly for over two hours, by which time it was 15 feet clear of the bottom. Then expanding air reached its full force and in less than 30 seconds the bow rushed to the surface with the usual spectacular effect. The most dangerous experience was that of the men on top of the airlocks who had been registering pressures, degree of list etc only a few feet above sea level and now found themselves clinging to precarious perches 120 feet in the air. *Bertha* hummed with activity as wires were paid out or hove in, pipe lines slackened and compressors switched to other compartments as required. So efficiently was everything organised that in less than a minute after the bow had broken surface, the ship was stable.

The bulkheads, however, had suffered badly from the quick alterations in pressure and the terrific expansion of air, while the slowness at which pressures were increased by the compressors disclosed a leakage of air which it took all the next day to make good. Then, at 13.00 hrs two days later, a slight movement was followed by the unexpected rush of the stern to the surface. *Kaiserin* then levelled out, and in two hours had 14 feet freeboard fore and aft, and was quite stable. Next day she was grounded in 12 fathoms, the superstructure, funnels and turrets were blasted away, and a few days later she was taken to Lyness to prepare her for her upside-down tow to Rosyth where she was docked beside the remains of *König Albert*.

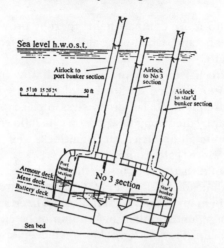

Cross section through No 3 main section

Plan showing arrangement of sections

Figure 6. Kaiserin – *cross-section and subdivision.*

Nine months' hard work on *Friedrich der Grosse* began in June 1936. During the internment she had been the flagship of Vice-Admiral von Reuter who had taken exceptionally thorough measures before she was sunk. She was distinguishable from other ships of her class by a heavy foremast.

Her charted position was known and she was soon located on fairly soft bottom in 23 fathoms with a heavy port list of 16 degrees. The extent of the list and the fact that she was four degrees down by the stern presented many engineering difficulties, and it was immediately clear that the only practicable method of lifting her again was by the use of compressed air. The first of ten air-locks was in place at the beginning of July. Their construction was precisely the same as before, and the greater number enabled Metal Industries to divide the bunker sections into more compartments thereby providing better control over list and stability. The air-locks varied from 80 to 100 feet in length.

The acute list created problems in fixing the air-locks. Weather often delayed the work, and even in good weather divers had frequently to lash themselves in place to avoid being carried away by the strong tidal stream which flowed across the wreck. Despite all obstacles, all ten airlocks were secured just before the winter gales commenced.

Months of difficult work inside the ship were then spent in making bulkheads tight. Divers found every valve in the ship open, and in many cases valve spindles had been sawn off flush with packing glands so that they could not be closed. All too often, also, clips on watertight doors had been sawn off. Many doors were missing and never found, which indicated that they must have been removed and thrown overboard at the time of scuttling.

Davie Bell, one of the men working below, came up with a grisly story. He declared that he had found the dungeon where sailors had been left to die by their officers, and that the place was littered with human bones. Floating weeds had added to the eerie atmosphere and he had the uneasy feeling all the time he was working that the ship was haunted. A prompt examination soon revealed that the dungeon was the ship's refrigeration room, and the bones were the remains of hams and legs of mutton.

By the third week in April 1937 the bulkheads were airtight and McKenzie was commenting on the cheerfulness with which divers had worked under circumstances of grave risk, while inside the ship men in wading dresses had again worked almost up to their necks in water. Many seemingly impossible tasks had been successfully completed at the second or third attempt, while some simple tasks which would not have occupied more than a few minutes on the surface had taken days to complete.

On 28 April at 05.00 hrs, the compressors were started and the lift began. It had all been seen several times before: the slow, inch-by-inch lifting of the bow for the first two feet, then the eruption at the water's surface as the superstructure tore free of mud and silt, the cascading of water off the weed-covered

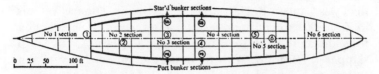

Diagram 7. Friedrich der Grosse: *plan showing arrangement of sections.*

bottom; the gigantic oily bubbles and the huge spouts of water, mud and oil; salvage ships rolling heavily in the turbulence, and *Bertha's* deck awash for a few seconds; the quick subsidence of the turmoil, and the laughter and cheers of relief as five minutes later the bow lay quietly on the surface.

The forward air-locks which had previously shown only ten to 15 feet above water now towered 120 feet in the air.

The stern was lightened to prevent crushing, and at 21.00 hrs work was discontinued, except for maintaining pressures until 05.00 hrs the following day when pumping at full power began again. An hour after noon the stern rose to the surface in 40 seconds, creating the inevitable turbulence, but though the ships rolled and sheered, and the wires strained tight, nothing broke, and within an hour *Friedrich der Grosse* lay flat with 12 feet of freeboard. After divers had surveyed the underside of the wreck, she was towed to shallow water off Risa where her superstructure was blasted away. Ten days later she was towed to Lyness, and having been prepared for her bottom-up tow, proceeded in charge of three Dutch tugs and Metal Industries' salvage tug, *Metinda,* to the breakers' yard at Rosyth.

The departure from Lyness received full honours from the vessels which witnessed it and from the workshops at Lyness. Whistles and sirens blew. A Blue Funnel liner, salvage steamers, the Admiralty's boom defence ships, and even the curious locomotives on Orkney's only railway system combined to give the departing ship a worthy farewell. Everything that had steam blew, except *Bertha,* lying in Bring Deeps, and the famous pontoon which lay at anchor temporarily out of use. *Friedrich der Grosse* acknowledged the salute with a resonant note on her great bell, which had been hung on her keel for the occasion, and the Dutch tugs saluted with deep notes on their sirens.

The tugs were admired by all. The commodore of the small

fleet was Captain B. Hart in *Thames*. Captain Thomas Vet was in *Zwarte Zee*, the most powerful tug in the world. She was 792 tons and built at Rotterdam in 1933. Captain A. van Dorp skippered *Roode Zee*. With them were Engineer Heer W. van Beelen, superintendent for L. Smit & Co of Rotterdam, the firm which had towed 80 floating docks to different parts of the world, and Heer J.P. Bruynzeel, a travelling student. *Roode Zee* and *Thames* were being used for the first time.

But no sooner had they left the islands than *Friedrich der Grosse* was caught by the 'race'. Tugs lashed the sea with their propellers in an attempt to maintain speed, and the heavy towing chains were heaved out of the water. *Zwarte Zee*, which could develop 4,000 horsepower and a speed of 20 knots, was keeling over as the speed increased, but the tugs could not hold the enormous mass of metal which, pulled by the ebb tide, was drawn back, hauling the tugs with her. The sea swirled around, exposing the great hulk's triple screws as she swung slowly round, edging her way broadside on to the rocks under John o' Groats. For the next half hour she was swept to and fro. The intended direction was east, but until 13.30 hrs they were travelling west, the tugs groaning and straining in vain to hold her. At last the tide turned and the sea began to surge from the Atlantic, and almost abruptly *Friedrich der Grosse* gave up her wayward struggle and began moving towards the North Sea of her own accord without the aid of the tugs, so powerful was the tide. For a time the tugs had little more to do than keep her headed through the passage. After three days a stiff breeze blew across the North Sea, and heavy seas creamed over the heaving hulk. Air was lost out of her and the speed fell to three knots, but the holes inside were sealed and for the next 11 days she behaved perfectly, and the crew of 12 living aboard her in the bunkhouse strapped to her keel had little to do but fool about. It took six hours for her to shoot the Firth of Forth; once she scraped the stonework but was pushed off by *Zwarte Zee*, and at last she was safely moored, on 5 August 1937.

After she was dry-docked, 200 men were employed in breaking her up. There had recently been increases in the prices of scrap-metal and the value of her hull was now assessed at more than £130,000.

So many ships had now been raised that when *Grosser Kurfürst* was refloated on 29 April 1938 by similar means, little publicity was given to the feat. (Incidentally, several steel plates used in the liner *Queen Mary* were forged from the scrap metal of *Grosser Kurfürst.*) The lift was perfect, by far the best of anything that had gone before, and there was nothing spectacular about it. Her superstructure lay embedded in the blue clay which forms the floor of Scapa Flow. One of her sections formed almost the whole bow and another the whole stern. Of her decks, the first, nearest the keel and working from keel to superstructure, was a double-bottom tank containing the trimming tanks; the second was the lower platform deck containing the pump-room, stores etc, the third, the upper platform deck, contained the magazines; the fourth was the armour or protective deck; the fifth, the mess deck; the sixth, the battery deck; finally there was an overdeck, or top deck, containing six-inch guns and casemate guns.

More than two miles of two-inch salvage piping were in use, and in the wreck were 383 yards of air piping and a similar length of three-quarter-foot air piping. Connected to the air-locks were four miles of wires. One worker said that down below on a sunny day he could read small print 20 fathoms below by the daylight filtering down through her portholes.

The craft in attendance were the tugs *Bertha, Metinda* and *Monarch,* also *Mary Cowie,* the motor cabin cruiser *Doris* and the pontoon ship *Never Die. Never Die* was ugly but reliable, a vessel without bow or stern. She was moored off the bow of the wreck, connected to her by a hawser. A big derrick on her pointed skywards, and she sat slightly on her heel, for water had been pumped into the stern tanks to augment the pontoon's bow resistance to the wreck. Hawsers were made fast between the raised bow of the wreck, the pontoon and *Bertha,* to prevent the hulk when it rose from moving further from, or nearer to, *Bertha,* for to have done so would have snapped the air-lines. The blow of escaping air when the stern rose tended to push *Bertha* away, and both bow and stern hawsers had to be light enough for men to be able to operate them within seconds of receiving orders, yet strong enough to keep the air-lines from parting and depriving the wreck of its means of buoyancy. *Bertha* pumped in free air at the rate of 2,350 cubic feet per minute and *Metinda* at 1,000 cubic feet per minute.

The bow lifted gently when she came up, and to inform the depot of their success, a kite was flown from the diving boat where Cowan, the chemist, stood by.

Every man had his eye on a watch when the lift was made, for there was a raffle on the time she would surface, which was exactly 12.54½ hrs. There was remarkably little seaweed or other marine growths on her as she had lain in a strong tideway.

At the banquet and dance to celebrate the success of the lift, an event instituted by Metal Industries Ltd, a parody composed by Max Wilkinson, a senior executive, was greatly appreciated by those whose working lives depended upon air pressure:

> Ol' man Pressure, dat ol' man Pressure,
> He must know sumpin', but don't say nothin',
> He keeps wreck raisin',
> He keeps on pressin' along.

> He don't plant taters, lie don't grow cotton,
> But all that meet him do feel rotten,
> Body all achin' and mighty tender.
> Just a little twinge and you lands in chamber.

> Ol' man Pressure, dat ol' man Pressure,
> He may bust sumpin', but don't say nothin'
> He keeps wreck raisin',
> He keeps on pressin' along.

Salvage operations ended just before World War II with the raising of *Derfflinger*, described by McKenzie as the most difficult and interesting case of all those lifted. She had taken part in the bombardment of Scarborough. At Jutland she had been badly punished and had lost more than 150 men. She lay, too, the deepest of all to the north-west of Cava, upside-down and listing 20 degrees, with 90 feet of water over her at high tide on one side and 110 feet on the other. This was twice the depth from which *Moltke* had been raised. Her nine air-locks had therefore to be positioned deeper than any others which had been made, and the longest was 130 feet, weighing 30 tons, complete with fittings, ladders, guys etc. After 20 years on the bottom *Derfflinger* was deep in mud. Work began in July 1938. In the early stages the list was so steep that men had literally to slide to work on her. Scaling and patching occupied eight months. On McKenzie's advice she was partitioned into 11 sealed sections. Men inside the hull had to work at a pressure of 64 pounds to the square inch and they needed one and a half hours of decompression after each hourly shift, a time to which they were limited each day.

The air-locks were secured in the same way as with previous ships with relays of six or eight divers who took from four to six hours to secure each air-lock. Water inside the ship was expelled by compressed air. When the ship's bottom was dry, access to the double-bottom tank was obtained through a manhole drilled and cut in the bottom plating. The bottom of the air-lock shaft and the ship's plating were then immediately sealed. If the tank lid of the double bottom was open, increasing pressure of air would cause the water in the tank to recede slowly but, if the tank was sealed, the pressure in the air-lock began to build up, something which had to be watched carefully as the Germans had arranged for the ships to capsize when scuttled by pumping and scaling many of the double-bottom tanks. When, therefore, the tank lid was found to be sealed, water in the tank was expelled through specially fitted valves until the lid could be located and opened.

Nine shafts were fitted, giving access to different sections of the ship. This division of the ship into sections gave the water in her different compartments a stepping effect, and provided better control over list and trim when the wreck was buoyant.

The method of work adopted was as follows: the first shift went down and completed its shift of one hour, whereupon it was relieved by the second shift. The first shift then entered the top chamber of the air-lock and began decompression. The lower chamber was then free for the second shift on completion of their working time. When the first shift completed decompression, it left the top chamber of the lock which was now free for the third shift to enter. Pressures in the top and lower chambers were then equalised so that the third shift could pass down, and the second shift move up to the top chamber. When men of the second shift had completed decompression, they left the air-lock, so that two chambers were now available as required for the third shift.

After the bow was raised pressures were adjusted in the various sections to control any list. Divers then went down to check whether the turrets had lifted with the ship or were still on the bottom. Had they fallen out, as was the case with *Bayern*, the weight would have been reduced by some 2,500 tons, thus raising the centre of gravity by about two feet four inches, which under certain conditions could have made the ship unstable. The divers' reports were satisfactory, so compressed air was pumped into the stern at the rate of 4,000 to 5,000 cubic feet per minute. Then pressure in the after sections was slowly increased until positive buoyancy was obtained. The volume of air in the stern and its resultant expansion was lower than in the bow, but it was sufficient to drive down the bow to a dangerously low level owing to rapid compression forward as the ship levelled out on the surface. To counteract this, all the available compressing power was switched to the bow section when the first upward movement of the stern was seen. Thereafter it was comparatively easy to control both list and trim, as all bulkheads had successfully withstood heavy pressures caused by rapid alterations in pressure as the ship lifted. The foredeck, however, which was the weakest part, especially under internal pressure, was blown completely out by expanding air. At first she rose only two feet a minute and then, as pressure decreased, the rusty hull rose 150 feet into the air creating the semblance of a sub-marine volcanic eruption. That many bulkheads withstood pressures and strains for which they were never designed was a tribute to German naval construction. Pressures were then balanced and divers went down to blast away all loose parts of the super-structure dragging on the bottom. When clear, she was towed inshore and grounded in 60 feet of water, and moored there with eight seven and a half-ton anchors, two off each bow and two off each quarter. Several weeks of reclamation work followed. Bulkheads were sealed down to still lower levels, casements were sealed up, and every aperture on the ship's side from keel to battery deck was effectively sealed to gain buoyancy and raise the ship to maximum level. Then gauges were passed under the superstructure to check the draught at the lowest points. Forty feet three inches was recorded at the forward super (A) turret, 40 feet four inches at the conning tower and 39 feet nine inches at the after super turret. War being imminent, the Admiralty required Rosyth dry dock for more important work, so *Derfflinger* was towed behind Risa Island and moored there with ten seven and a half-ton anchors.

Between 1924 and 1939, 38 ships had been raised and 327,000 tons of steel recovered and broken up.

In the early days of the war, when *Derfflinger* lay moored alongside *Iron Duke*, at that time a training ship, three German aircraft appeared. At first they were not fired upon so as not to disclose the strength of the defences. But *Iron Duke* was holed and water flooded her compartments. McKenzie immediately went out to her, and it was his prompt advice and assistance which prevented her from sinking. Meanwhile, anti-aircraft guns had opened fire. One aircraft was brought down, all that was found of its pilot being a foot in a boot and an arm in a sleeve.

The Admiralty had no salvage organisation at the outbreak of war and, apart from a few pumps and other obsolescent equipment in various dockyards, had no salvage resources of any kind. The heads of existing salvage organisations were therefore allocated areas in which they agreed to be responsible for salvage and for full co-operation with the Admiralty. Metal Industries, for example, was allocated the northern area, covering the waters from Cape Wrath to the Moray Firth and the Orkney, Shetland and Faroe Islands. As soon as possible the Admiralty then formed its own salvage department under the direction of Commodore, later Rear-Admiral, A.R. Dewar. When planning for the invasion of Europe began, McKenzie's ability was rated so highly that in January 1944 he was appointed Principal Salvage Officer, North-West Europe, on the staff of Admiral Sir Bertram Ramsay, Allied Naval Commander-in-Chief, Expeditionary Force. McKenzie was commissioned in the rank of Commodore RNVR and was subsequently decorated with the orders of the CB and CBE. For his work in clearing Dutch canals of obstructions, the Dutch government also appointed him an officer of the Order of William.

For seven long years throughout the war and well into peacetime, *Derfflinger* lay bottom up, kept afloat by a small maintenance party who lived for the whole time in a hut built on the ship's bottom. No other ship has ever remained so long afloat upside-down.

In 1946, after raising *Derfflinger* about 70 feet because of her funnels and superstructure, she was prepared for the tow to Rosyth. The hull was reasonably watertight, and to replace lost air it was merely necessary to operate compressors two or three times a week for two or three hours at a time. The compressing plant was in the company's vessels *Bertha, Metinda* and *Imperious.* But the Admiralty now needed their dry dock at Rosyth, and Metal Industries had to find another place to dispose of her. About this time the Admiralty had for disposal a surplus, 40-year-old, 30,000-ton floating dock. Metal Industries bought it to tow *Derfflinger* in it to the Clyde, where she was eventually docked at Faslane Port.

But floating docks are not designed to carry ships upside-down. McKenzie, writing of *Derfflinger's* unequal distribution of weight, said:

> There can be no question of carrying the *Derfflinger* mainly along the centre line as the two turrets and the two turret rings were the lowest points capable of carrying a heavy load, and had the load been concentrated on these points it would certainly have wrecked the dock. After careful study and calculations it was decided to rest the ship lightly on the forward turret, on B turret barbette ring, the port and starboard plating of a heavy tank-like structure near midships, parts of the midship deck structure, the after super turret barbette ring, the after turret, and on 50 or more nests of blocks and/or shores under the casemates and other strong points along the ship's side.

The various heights necessary were calculated from drawings and the divers had to fit only the capping blocks. Chain cable was used as ballast for each nest of blocks in such a way that buoyancy was just negative. This enabled blocks to be left in position yet easily movable by divers.

Perhaps the most intricate work connected with this part of the salvage operations was getting *Derfflinger* into dry dock, for the dock had to be sunk eight feet below its normal maximum working depth, and even so *Derfflinger* would have only six feet freeboard to the top of the dock walls or side tanks, and there was still only six inches clearance over the blocks at the lowest points. Moreover, the margin of stability was low, so that air pressures in the various sections had to be delicately balanced lest the ship should settle and foul the dock bottom while being manoeuvred into the required position. This work was successfully accomplished and, as the pressure was reduced, the ship settled firmly on the pre-selected points.

The work of blocking up went hand-in-hand with the difficult and delicate task of exactly maintaining the ship's level. Six divers completed the blocking up in just over four weeks. McKenzie declared that only a team of first-class divers could have carried out this work successfully. Then, in just over 24 hours, the dock was slowly raised by pumping until its deck was above water level. The repair department of the firm of Alexander Stephen & Sons Ltd assisted Metal Industries with this operation. W.B. Johnstone, a director of this firm, considered that the greatest difficulty experienced in the control of the dock during the docking and lifting was in judging the exact amount of water in the tanks. The Navy had apparently decided that piping between the tanks and radiators were of no importance as they had corroded away. The only method of checking the amount of water in the double-bottom tanks after the dock was submerged was to wait until the dock floor emerged from the water, then remove a manhole door and check the height of water in the tank. When lifting a vessel on to a floating dock the main principle is to watch the breakage, or bending, that takes place during the whole lifting procedure. The dock must be kept as straight as possible, and for a dock of the length of the one used, no more than three inches of breakage is acceptable. Surprisingly the gauge fitted by the Admiralty for checking the breakage was on the floor of the dock and could therefore only be watched and recorded after the vessel had been lifted. Special water gauge pipes were therefore run along the dock walls, and a theodolite was placed at one end of the dock to keep a check on the breakage during the lifting operation but, as darkness fell, chances had to be taken during the final lift. Another disturbing feature was the bad riveting in several tanks midships and, before the operation could begin, some 4,000 bolts had to be fished through the bottom of the dock so that the leaky tanks could be made watertight in order to give the maximum lifting capacity. J. Robertson and McGillvray, whose responsibility it was to mark off the dock bottom, fix blocks etc, had only a small scale drawing, all in German, to work from, for the Admiralty seemed to have very few drawings available and these were far from accurate.

The most difficult part of the work now lay behind them, but what remained was still far from easy. As the six-ton quayside cranes were inadequate for the task, a 60-ton floating crane was bought from the Ministry of Transport to operate on the seaward side of the dock. The projecting ends of the ship were removed, and on each end of the dock, derrick-cranes of 12-ton capacity which could be moved on rails were erected. On the dock walls were three-ton and five-ton cranes which were used to move material within their capacity. After the ship had been cut down to the armour deck level, sheer legs were erected on the deck and the great main armour plates, each weighing from 20 to 30 tons, were lowered on to a steel truck specially built for the task on the dock's deck. The truck then moved along a railway track which had been laid to the end of the dock where the armour plates were lifted off by the floating crane.

In just over 15 months *Derfflinger* was completely reduced to 20,000 tons of scrap, and soon afterwards Metal Industries sold the dock to foreign buyers, having no further use for it themselves.

Derfflinger was the last ship of the German fleet to be raised. The battleships *Kronprinz Wilhelm, Markgraf* and *König* lay in the deep channel between Cava and Barrel of Butter in 22 to 25 fathoms with lists of 30 to 40 degrees, though the lists were slowly decreasing as their upperworks subsided into the mud, and the light cruisers *Cöln, Karlsruhe* and *Brummer* lay too deep to be dealt with economically. So Metal Industries accepted the conclusion reached by their experts that any ship in 30 or more fathoms of water could be written off as an economic salvage operation except for the recovery of a valuable cargo, and abandoned them.

The Admiralty then decided to use Scapa Flow once more as a base for the Home Fleet, and these last few enemy ships were left to rust away. But at the end of World War II events occurred which completely altered the scrap value of steel in the remaining wrecks. These were the atomic explosions in Japan, which resulted in contamination of the atmosphere by fall-out. This has meant that *all* steels made after 1945 are to a very slight extent radioactive. However, the level of radioactivity is one of the very lowest, and substantially below any form of health hazard. Nevertheless it is still high enough to disturb the most delicate of radioactive detectors. Now steel is required for shielding radioactive detectors from background radiation. Other materials, such as lead, are not suitable, for they frequently have naturally occurring activity. Moreover, furnace lining thicknesses are sometimes tested by the use of radio-isotopes which add still further to the activity level in steel. Large quantities of air, either as air or as oxygen, are required in the making of every ton of steel, and it therefore follows that for the most sensitive shielding experiments, pre-1945 steel is essential, and the scarcity value of such steel of a thickness of two and a half inches or more became double the value of steel manufactured after 1945.

Shipbreaking Industries Ltd profited by this when breaking up the armoured decks of HMS *Vanguard* and several other ships whose steel fulfilled the requisite specifications. It is believed that the only remaining main sources of thick, pre-1946 steel are the first HMS *Vanguard,* HMS *Royal Oak* in Scapa Flow, probably a few obsolete South American fighting ships and the battlecruiser *Goeben* which was obtained by Turkey on 16 August 1914, renamed *Jawuz Sultan Selim* and in 1936 again renamed *Yavuz.* Turkey is still trying to sell this vessel, which will in all probability eventually be reduced to scrap by foreign shipbreakers.

But the last few survivors of the scuttled fleet were not to be left undisturbed, for Mr Arthur Nundy, owner of a marine salvage company known as Nundy (Marine Metals) Ltd, acquired the hulks. He made no attempt to raise any of the vessels. In any case they lay at too great a depth for sustained effort by divers. *Markgraf* lay in 45 metres of water, *König* in 40 metres and *Kronprinz Wilhelm* in 35–40 metres, and the cruisers *Cöln, Karlsruhe* and *Brummer* at varying depths. Nundy therefore concentrated upon blasting open their bottoms and taking out piecemeal any side armour, armoured decks and non-ferrous metals he could recover by a combination of skin-diving and helmet-diving, the former bearing a higher proportion to the latter than is usual. He was particularly interested in thick steel free from radioactivity, which is essential for certain types of surgical apparatus, for example, for screens and machines used in the treatment of cancer.

A skin diver cannot safely descend to a depth of more than 120 feet without needing a stop for decompression on the way up again. At this depth, as had been stated before, the blood soon becomes saturated with dissolved gases, including nitrogen, and carries them to various parts of the body where they are absorbed at different rates depending upon the organ. For example, cartilages and tendons have a poor blood supply, and it therefore takes a long time for them to absorb the gases. But it also takes a very long time for these parts of the body to release their dissolved gases back into the bloodstream when the diver begins his ascent. The inert gases, such as nitrogen, cause decompression sickness. If the diver surfaces too quickly, then the gases come out of solution, due to the decreasing pressure. while still trapped in particular parts of the body such as knee-joints and elbows – hence the 'bends'. Ruptured lung tissue can also be caused by air embolism if a diver surfaces too quickly.

It is to be regretted that Mr Nundy has been reluctant to disclose the nature of his work, but it is said that his divers descended to about 70 feet quickly, placed explosive charges and quickly surfaced again. Then another quick dive to attach slings and grabs, followed by another quick surfacing. Nundy ceased operations as soon as the work became unprofitable and, as there is no longer any possibility of the hulks being lifted, it would seem that the last chapter has been written on the greatest salvage operation of all time.

The main credit for the salvage of the German fleet belongs to Cox and McCrone who provided the capital and initiative for embarking upon the work and accepted responsibility for its success or failure, and to McKenzie, upon whose skill and ability both relied. Professor A.M. Robb, DSc, when vice-president of the Institution of Engineers and Shipbuilders in Scotland, in paying tribute to McKenzie's work, said:

In addition to the supervision of an immense amount of detail, there are the larger problems which demand that the salvage officer must be a bit of a naval architect and a bit of an engineer: there are some tricky problems in naval architecture involved in the use of compressed air. To have the qualities of a naval architect and an engineer is very desirable, but there is something even more important – the possession of that invaluable but indefinable quality recognised as 'savvy'.

APPENDIX 1

Vice-Admiral von Reuter's Account of the Scuttling

Extract from Vice-Admiral Ludwig von Reuter's book, *Scapa Flow – Das Grab der deutscher Flotte*, published in Leipzig, 1921.

As usual, two English communications ships (*Signalverbindung*) lay alongside (the *Emden*), also another vessel which had begun to pump a supply of water into the *Emden*'s tanks. Had I made known the order (to sink), the natural excitement of the *Emden*'s crew could not have been concealed from the crews of these vessels. They would have raised the alarm, recalled the English Admiral, and obstructed the sinking of the other ships.

Shortly after 12 o'clock, *Friedrich der Grosse* began to list more and more as she sank deeper; her boats had already been lowered and lay by the stern. Now, loud and clear, from her bell came single notes – the signal 'abandon ship'. We watched the crew climb into boats, and the boats being lowered. *Friedrich der Grosse* heeled over still further. Water streamed through her open ports. After a few minutes she turned over and sank to the depths. The air forced through her funnels created two great eddies of water. Then all was silent. The time was 16 minutes past 12.

The bell seemed to have vitalised all the other ships as though this was the signal for which they had been waiting. Everywhere the activity increased. Here boats were being lowered to the water, there crews were dragging their heavy kitbags to the bulwarks. Elsewhere boats were being manned and were putting off to loud cheers from the crews. An English guard-ship, which had for some time lain near *Friedrich der Grosse*, and may have noticed her exceptional list with concern and excitement, was puzzled by the bell signal and the resultant manning of the boats. When the giant ship suddenly overturned and sank before their eyes, they were so shocked that they lost their heads and opened a wild fire on the unarmed and defenceless occupants of the boats, although the latter were waving the white flag. At the same time they also sounded their siren. Its urgent wail startled the crews of the other English guard-ships out of their lethargy – understandable enough on a warm summer morning when their admiral was away. As is customary when a coarse people experience a rapid change from idyllic peace to extreme excitement, they lost their heads and blindly vented their rage upon everything which seemed to them contrary to the normal state of affairs.

Their panic spread to the English destroyers which had remained behind in harbour. Under its effect such cruelties were perpetrated on the defenceless German crews that England is robbed of any right to express indignation against German war criminals. It was fortunate that the sinking of *Friedrich der Grosse* was quickly followed by that of *König Albert, Moltke* and *Brummer*; others were approaching their end. The number of boats drifting with shipwrecked sailors grew so fast that the English vessels in their confusion did not seem to know upon which boat they should fire first. So they turned quickly from one to another, and it is due to this constant change that greater mischief was not wrought.

The end of *Friedrich der Grosse* and also of *Brummer* which lay astern of *Emden*, had also excited the English vessels lying alongside the latter. As the crew of *Emden* were dining below deck, they had noticed nothing of events in the harbour, but now it was time to order the sinking of *Emden* also. Under the direction of the commanding officer, the valves and underwater broadside tubes were opened and the water poured in. One of the English communications vessels, probably from fear of being sucked down into the depths by *Emden*, tried to disengage. I gave orders, however, that it was to be kept attached to *Emden* until the latter's crew were safely aboard it.

As the English fire upon the German boats continued without slackening despite the hoisting of white flags, I decided to visit the English admiral ashore to induce him to order a cease-fire. As I was unaware of the position of his official HQ and of the boat landing point I boarded with my staff the other English communications ship, one which was held ready for my visits. It landed us in a rock-strewn bay. We had seen from a distance that a car was racing up at top speed. In it sat a young man wearing tennis gear. The captain of the drifter referred to him as the Shore CO. He seemed to me to be very young. I begged him to order cease-fire. He was dreadfully excited, and scarcely listened and certainly did not understand a single word of mine. He ran off, to return shortly afterwards with a camera. Then he jumped into a waiting speed-boat and roared out of the bay. I assumed that he would order a cease-fire, but I was disappointed in this. The English drifter was to take us back to *Emden*. It was an ebb tide, and as we steered out of the bay we got stuck on a sandbank. Even with my personal assistance all efforts failed to get the heavy, clumsy boat afloat. The hills along the bay blocked our view of the ships. Only my admiral's flag on *Emden* was visible – it just refused to disappear! For probably an hour we were stuck on the sandbank cut off from world events; at last, with the turn of the tide, we drifted free and could sail out of the bay.

And what a scene it was! Before us, *Grosser Kurfürst* rose sharply into the air. With a racket both anchor chains parted, and the ship listed to port and capsized, the red paint on her bottom glaring across the blue sea. Many anchorages were by this time forsaken for the journey to the sea-bed.

English destroyers tore into the bay with foam at their bows. One of them drew alongside *Emden* and tried to blow up the anchor-chain in order to tow her into shallow water. As *Emden* sank deeper, I ordered the drifter to change course from *Emden* and steer for *Bayern* whose crew, lying and sitting on rescue buoys, were drifting near their ship. We took them on board and immediately *Bayern* turned over with water streaming through her open ports. In a few minutes the bulkheads were flooded, and the giant ship capsized and sank, the German flag still flying and the crew honouring her last voyage with three cheers. Now there was borne to us on the light wind the sound of salvoes from English destroyers which sought to halt the work of destruction on our cruisers. A tough battle was being fought out there. Once again the spirit of war arose in those magnificent officers and men who had no weapons to help them – only their sense of duty. And so, despite heavy fire from the enemy destroyers and guard-vessels, they carried on with their work of destruction. Six Flotilla which suffered especially had received the signal at an unfavourable moment when the English had recovered their nerve. Of 50 ships, 46 were sunk, a great performance! As I tried to reach them, English ships of the line rushed into the bay at top speed, ready for battle, their 38 centimetre guns aimed at the remnant of my unit. It was time for me to visit the English admiral and effect the cessation of hostile action. The fire weakened and was gradually stilled. In the background, the great cruisers were in their death-throes: *Seydlitz* capsized; the bulkheads and forecastles of *Derfflinger* and *von der Tann* were already flooded. They would soon be finished. Only *Hindenburg* lay flat upon the water, but she was settling. I recalled that her commanding officer wanted to sink her on an even keel. Of the ships of the line, only *Baden*, with a list, and *Markgraf*, apparently intact, were above water. *Emden* was afloat, also *Nürnberg*. *Frankfurt* seemed on the point of sinking. Then *Bremse*, under tow by English destroyers, foundered. Her brave captain, First Lieutenant Schacke, managed to sink her, even though his ship was now manned by a British crew. During my journey to the English flagship, more boats containing rescued men were taken in tow.

I was deeply moved and full of gratitude to my brave officers and crew who had carried out their orders so brilliantly. All these magnificent battleships and destroyers had gone, sunk, once the pride of the German nation, mighty works of German shipbuilding skill. How much thought, how much military skill and experience had gone into them! Development without parallel had been concluded and lay sunk in the grave.

The English flagship had just anchored. Turmoil seethed around her – patrol boats, drifters, guard-ships, naval boats – all crowded in, anxious to present their reports: that the German fleet had gone to its grave. At last my drifter succeeded in getting through and tying up. A ladder was dropped over the side for me. I went aboard the *Revenge* and was received by the English Vice-Admiral, Sir Sydney R. Fremantle.

APPENDIX 2

Secret Letter Found in Cabin Safe in SMS Emden

Letter from Admiral von Trotha, chief of German Admiralty, found in cabin safe of Vice-Admiral von Reuter in SMS *Emden*. Published in a statement by the British Admiralty.

From Chief of the Admiralty   Berlin, 9 May 1919

No. A 111 5332   <u>Most Secret</u>

Sir, – You have repeatedly expressed to Commander Stapenhorst the wish of the interned ships to be informed as to their fate and the probable termination of their internment. The fate of this, the most valuable part of our fleet, will probably be finally decided in the negotiations for a preliminary peace, now being carried on. From Press news and utterances in the British House of Lords, it appears that our opponents are considering the idea of depriving us of the interned ships on the conclusion of peace; they waver between the destruction or the distribution among themselves of these ships. The British naturally raise some doubts about the latter course. These hostile intentions are in opposition to the hitherto unquestioned German right of ownership of the vessels, with the internment of which we complied on the conclusion of the armistice only because we were obliged to consent, for the duration of the armistice, to an appreciable weakening of the striking power of the German fleet. This assumption was freely expressed, and was not contradicted by the enemy, either at the conclusion of the armistice or on its prolongation. We, on the other hand, have often repeated this interpretation, when we protested in February, 1919, against the unjustified internment in an enemy harbour, designating this to be a contravention of the terms of the armistice and demanding the subsequent removal of the ships to a neutral harbour; this protest, it is true, remained unanswered. Sir, you may rest assured that it will be no more than the plain duty of our Naval Delegates at Versailles to safeguard the fate of our interned ships in every way, and to arrive at a solution which is in accordance with our traditions and our unequivocal German rights. In this connection, the first condition will be that the ships remain German, and that their fate, whatever turn it may take under the pressure of the political situation, will not be decided without our co-operation, and will be consumated by ourselves, and that their surrender to the enemy remains out of the question. We must hope that these just demands may retain their position in the scheme of our political standpoint in the question of peace as a whole. I beg you, Sir, as far as possible to express to the officers and crews of the interned ships my satisfaction that, for their part, they are so eagerly nursing our most natural hope, that the interned ships will be retained under the German flag, and to communicate to them our strong desire to make your just cause triumphant. This spirit is calculated to support the German Delegates in their efforts at the Peace Conference. The fate of the whole Navy will depend upon the results of these efforts; it is to be hoped that they will put an end to the internment which, through our enemies' breach of faith, has become so cruel, the sufferings and trials of which are deplored by our whole Navy, and which will ever be remembered to the credit of the interned crews.

To the Commander-in-Chief of the Interned Ships,
Rear Admiral von Reuter, Scapa Flow.

APPENDIX 3

Analysis of Scrap from Break-up of SMS Friedrich der Grosse

	Tonnage	Price			Value
Ferrous		£	s	d	£
Steel scrap	8281	3	6	8	27,603
Steel plates	253	5	0	0	1,265
Basic scrap	379	3	0	0	1,137
Wire rope	25	2	15	0	69
Nickel 3$^1/_2$ to 4% Chrome 1 to 2%	5979	8	10	0	50,822
Nickel 3 to 3$^1/_2$% Chrome 1 to 2%	615	7	10	0	4,612
Nickel bolts 5$^1/_2$ to 6%	30	12	0	0	360
Nickel 1 to 1$^1/_2$% Chrome $^1/_2$ to 1%	2853	4	10	0	12,838
Non-magnetic steel	3	39	10	0	118
Anchors and cables	48	3	15	0	180
Cast iron	287	4	0	0	1,148
Shafts	51	7	0	0	357
Boiler tubes	139	3	0	0	417
Nickel slag	—	—			—
	18,943				100,926
Non-Ferrous					
Condenser tubes	45	37	10	0	1,688
Condenser plates	4	30	0	0	120
Condenser ferrules	1	23	0	0	23
White metal	3	160	0	0	480
Brazing flanges	21	40	0	0	840
Spelter	6	11	0	0	66
Lead	52	14	0	0	728
Turbine blades	26	29	0	0	754
Brass	80	23	0	0	1,840
Nickel brass	5	21	10	0	108
Gunmetal	270	50	0	0	13,500
Electrical boxes	23	46	10	0	1,070
Copper	161	40	0	0	6,440
Manganese	70	22	0	0	1,540
Bronze	1	26	0	0	26
Cable ends	1	23	10	0	24
Resistance wire	1	23	0	0	23
Penny metal	1	40	10	0	41
Braziery metal	3	36	0	0	108
Armoured cable	—	—			—
	774				£29,419
Total	19,717				£130,345
Actual sales less carriage					£134,886

APPENDIX 4

Comparative Tables of Classes of German Warship at Scapa Flow

I BATTLESHIPS

Class	Standard Displacement Tons	Dimensions (feet)	Shaft Turbines	Machinery SHP	Machinery Knots	Machinery Firing	Protection (inches) Main Belt (ends)	Protection (inches) Main Belt (amid)	Protection (inches) Deck	Protection (inches) Turrets	Protection (inches) Fore Conning Tower	Armament	Complement
Kaiser	24,380	564 x 95 1/4 x 27 1/4	3	30,000 to 35,000	21 to 23	coal and oil	7 3/4	13 3/4	3	11 3/4	13 3/4	10 12-in, 14 5.9-in, 8 3.4-in guns, 4 3.4-in AA guns, 5 20-in torpedo tubes, (1 bow, 4 beam) all submerged.	1088
Note: Prinzregent Luitpold only 2-shaft geared turbines. SHP 26,000, 1-shaft diesel 12,000 BHP.													
König	25,390	580 x 97 x 28 1/2	3	31,000 to 35,000	21 to 23	coal and oil	10	14	4 1/2	14	14	10 12-in, 14 5.9-in, 8 3.4-in guns, 4 3.4-in AA guns, 5 20-in TT (1 bow 4 beam) all submerged.	1150
Baden	28,075	623 x 99 x 27 3/4	3	52,000	22 1/4	coal and oil	6	13 3/4	4 3/4	13 3/4	13 3/4	8 15-in, 16 5.9-in, 4 3.4-in guns, 4 3.4-in AA guns, 5 24-in TT (1 bow 4 beam) all submerged.	1200
von der Tann	19,400	562 3/4 x 87 x 27 1/2	4	43,600 to 80,000	28	coal	9 1/2	—	2 1/2	9	9	8 11-in, 10 5.9-in, 16 3.4-in guns, 4 18-in TT (1 bow 2 beam 1 stern) all submerged (4 3.4-in guns substituted for 3.4-in guns in 1916).	910
Moltke	22,640	610 x 96 3/4 x 27	4	70,000 to 80,000	27 to 28 1/2	coal	4	11	2 1/2	10	10	10 11-in, 12 5.9-in, 12 3.4-in guns 4 20-in TT (1 bow 2 beam 1 stern) all submerged.	1107

Class	Standard Displacement Tons	Dimensions (feet)	Shaft Turbines	SHP	Knots	Firing	Main Belt (ends)	Main Belt (amid)	Deck	Turrets	Fore Conning Tower	Armament	Complement
Seydlitz	24,610	606 x 93½ x 27	4	89,700	27 to 30	coal	4	11	2½	10	10	10 11-in, 12 5.9-in, 12 3.4-in guns*, 4 20-in TT (1 bow 2 beam 1 stern) all submerged.	1108
Derfflinger	26,180	689 x 95 x 27½	4	85,000	27 to 28	coal and oil	5	12	2½	11	11	8 12-in, 12 5.9-in (Hindenburg 14 5.9-in), 4 3.4-in (Derfflinger only), 8 3.4-in AA guns, 4 20-in TT (Hindenburg 4 24-in) (1 bow 2 beam 1 stern) all submerged.	1215

* Replaced in 1916 by 4.3-in AA guns

II CRUISERS

Class	Standard Displacement Tons	Dimensions (feet)	Shaft Turbines	SHP	Knots	Firing	Main Belt (ends)	Main Belt (amid)	Deck	Turrets	Fore Conning Tower	Armament	Complement
Bremse	4,400	460½ x 44 x 19½	2	47,000	28	coal and oil	—	1½	5/8	—	—	4 5.9-in and 2 3.4-in AA guns, 2 20-in (deck) TT, 400 mines.	309
Königsberg II	5,440	495½ x 47 x 21	2*	31,000	27 to 28	coal and oil	—	2½	¾	—	—	8 5.9-in and 2 3.4-in AA guns, 4 24-in TT (2 deck 2 submerged) 200 mines.	475
Dresden II	5,600	511½ x 47 x 21	2†	49,000	27 to 29	coal and oil	—	2–2½	¾	—	—	8 5.9-in and 3 3.4-in AA guns, 4 24-in (deck) TT, 200 mines.	559
Frankfurt	5,200	477 x 45½ x 19½	2†	31,000	27½	coal and oil	—	2½	¾	—	—	8 5.9-in and 2 3.4-in AA guns, 4 20-in TT (2 deck 2 submerged) 120 mines.	474

* Karlsruhe geared.
† geared.

Appendix 4

Class	Ships Scuttled	Standard Displacement Tons	Dimensions (feet)	Shaft Turbines	Machinery SHP	Machinery Knots	Firing	Armament	Complement
S31	S32, S36	802	261 x 27½ x 11	2	23,500 to 25,000	33 to 36	oil	3 3.4-in guns, 6 20-in TT, 24 mines.	83
G37	G38, G39, G40	822	261 x 27½ x 11	2	24,000 to 25,000	34	oil	As above.	83
V43	V43, V44, V45, V46	852	261 x 27½ x 11	2*	24,000 to 24,700	34 to 36	oil	As above.	87
S49	S49, S50, S51, S52	802	261 x 27½ x 11	2	24,000 to 25,000	34 to 36½	oil	As above.	83
S53	S53, S54, S55, S56, S60, S65	919	272½ x 27½ x 11½	2*	24,000 to 25,000	35 to 36	oil	S53, S54, S55, S56: 3 3.4-in guns. S60, S65: 3 4.1-in guns. All: 6 20-in TT, 24 mines.	87
V67	V70, V73, V78, V80, V81, V82, V83	924	269 x 27½ x 11½	2*	23,500 to 24,400	34 to 36½	oil	3 3.4-in guns, 6 20-in TT, 24 mines V82 and V83: 3 4.1-in guns; others later re-armed with 3 4.1-in guns.	87
G85	G86, G89, G91, G92	960	272¼ x 27½ x 11½	2	24,000 to 26,500	34	oil	3 3.4-in guns, 6 20-in TT, 24 mines G92: 3 4.1-in guns; others later re-armed with 3 4.1-in guns.	87
B97	B98	1374	321½ x 30½ x 12¼	2	36,000 to 40,000	35½ to 36½	oil	4 3.4-in guns, 6 20-in TT, 24 mines. 1916 re-armed with 4 4.1-in guns.	114
G101	G101, G102, G103, G104	1116	312¾ x 30½ x 12	2	28,000 to 29,500	33½	oil	As above.	104
B109	B109, B110, B111, B112	1374	321½ x 30½ x 12¼	2	40,000 to 40,700	36 to 37½	oil	As above.	114
V125	V125, V126, V127, V128, V129	924	269 x 27½ x 12½	2	23,500 to 25,150	34 to 34½	oil	3 4.1-in guns, 6 20-in TT, 24 mines.	105
S131	S131, S132, S136, S137, S138	919	272¾ x 27½ x 12½	2	23,700 to 24,000	33 to 34	oil	As above.	105
H145	H145	990	277 x 27½ x 12½	2	24,000	33½ to 34	oil	As above.	105
V99	V100	1350	324¾ x 30½ x 12¼	2	40,000 to 42,000	36½ to 37	oil	As above.	114

* Geared.

Note: The letter prefixes to the numbers denote the builders who were as follows: G – Germaniawerft, Kiel; V – A.G. Vulcan, Stettin (Hamburg in the case of Nos V70 and V83); S – Schickau, Elbing; H – Howaldtswerke, Kiel; B – Blohm and Voss, Hamburg.

APPENDIX 5

Ships of the German Fleet Interned in Scapa Flow

Ship	Class (see comparative tables)	Where built	Date launched	Time at which sank	Raised by	Date raised
Kaiser	Kaiser	Kiel D.Y.	22.3.11	13.25	Cox & Danks	20.3.29
Prinzregent Luitpold	Kaiser	Germaniawerft, Kiel	17.2.12	13.30	Cox & Danks	9.7.31
Kaiserin	Kaiser	Howaldtswerke, Kiel	21.6.09	14.00	Metal Industries	11.5.36
König Albert	Kaiser	Schickau, Danzig	27.4.12	12.54	Metal Industries	31.7.35
Friedrich der Grosse	Kaiser	A.G. Vulcan, Hamburg	10.6.11	12.16	Metal Industries	29.4.37
Bayern	Baden	Howaldtswerke, Kiel	18.2.15	14.30	Metal Industries	1.9.34
Grosser Kurfürst	König	A.G. Vulcan, Hamburg	5.5.13	13.30	Metal Industries	29.4.38

Salvage Abandoned

Ship	Class	Where built	Date launched	Time at which sank	Raised by	Date raised
Kronprinz Wilhelm	König	Germaniawerft, Kiel	21.2.14	13.15		
Markgraf	König	A.G. Weser, Bremen	4.6.13	16.45		
König	König	Wilhelmshaven D.Y.	1.3.13	14.00		

Ship	Class	Where built	Date launched	Time at which sank	Raised by	Date raised
Seydlitz	Seydlitz	Blohm & Voss, Hamburg	30.3.12	13.50	Cox & Danks	2.11.28
Moltke	Moltke	Blohm & Voss, Hamburg	4.7.10	13.10	Cox & Danks	10.6.27
von der Tann	von der Tann	Blohm & Voss, Hamburg	20.3.09	14.15	Cox & Danks	7.12.30

Appendix 5

Ship	Class (see comparative table)	Where built	Date launched	Time at which sank	Raised by	Date raised
Hindenburg	Derfflinger	Wilhelmshaven D.Y.	1.8.15	17.00	Cox & Danks	22.7.30
Derfflinger	Derfflinger	Blohm & Voss, Hamburg	(1) 14.6.13 unsuccessful (2) 12.7.13	14.45	Metal Industries	1939

Light Cruiser

Bremse	Bremse	A.G. Vulcan, Stettin	11.3.16	14.30	Cox & Danks	27.11.29

Abandoned

Cöln	Dresden II	Blohm & Voss, Hamburg	5.10.16	13.50		
Karlsruhe	Königsberg II	Wilhelmshaven D.Y.	31.1.16	15.50		
Brummer	Bremse	A.G. Vulcan, Stettin	11.12.15	13.05		
Dresden	Dresden II	Howaldtswerke, Kiel	25.4.17	15.30		

NOT SUNK

Battle Cruiser

Baden	Baden	Schickau, Danzig	30.10.15	Beached in Swanbister Bay in sinking condition. Finally sunk by R.N. as gunnery target off Portsmouth 16.8.21.

Light Cruiser

Emden	Königsberg II	A.G. Weser, Bremen	1.2.16	To France 11.3.20. Scrapped at Caen 1926.
Frankfurt	Frankfurt	Kiel D.Y.	20.3.15	Scuttled but beached. To USA, sunk 18.7.21 off Cape Henry, USA, in aerial bombing experiments.
Nürnberg	Königsberg II	Howaldtswerke, Kiel	14.4.16	Scuttled but mooring chains broke and drifted ashore.

Jutland to Junkyard

DESTROYERS

1. The distribution of destroyers among the flotillas is as listed by Vice-Admiral von Reuter.

2. All these ships were equipped with two-shaft turbines, and were oil-fired. They were armed with three 4.6-inch guns – replaced with 3.4-inch guns (except classes B97, G101 and B109 which had four 4.1-in guns), six 20-in torpedo tubes and 24 mines.

No.	Date launched	Lifted by	Date raised	Remarks
No. 1 Flotilla				
G40	27.2.15	Cox & Danks	29.7.25	
G86	24.8.15	Cox & Danks	14.7.25	
G39	16.1.15	Cox & Danks	3.7.25	
G38	23.12.14	Cox & Danks	27.9.24	
V129	21.6.19	Cox & Danks	11.8.25	
S32	28.2.14	Cox & Danks	19.6.25	
No. 2 Flotilla				
G101	12.8.14	Cox & Danks	13.4.26	Scuttled in shallow water. To
G102	16.9.14			USA 17.2.20 and sunk as target by bombing off Cape Henry.
G103	14.11.14	Cox & Danks	30.9.25	Foundered 11.25 in storm north of Scotland en route to breakers.
V100	8.3.15			Beached. To France where scrapped 1921.
B109	11.3.15	Cox & Danks	27.3.26	
B110	31.3.15	Cox & Danks	11.12.25	
B111	8.6.15	Cox & Danks	8.3.26	
B112	17.6.15	Cox & Danks	11.2.26	
G104	28.11.14	Cox & Danks	30.4.26	Not listed by von Reuter.
No. 3 Flotilla				
S53	18.9.15	Cox & Danks	13.8.24	
S54	11.10.15	Cox & Danks	5.6.25	
S55	6.11.15	Cox & Danks	29.8.24	
G91	16.11.15	Cox & Danks	12.9.24	
V70	14.10.15	Cox & Danks	1.8.24	Used as salvage hulk.
V73	24.9.15			Sunk in shallow water.
V81	27.5.16			Beached, sank en route to breakers.
V82	27.5.16			Beached.
No. 6 Flotilla				
V43	27.1.15			In shallow water. To USA. Sunk as target off Cape Henry.
V44	24.2.15			Salved by R.N.
V45	29.3.15			Salved by R.N.
V46	23.12.14			To France. Scrapped Cherbourg 1924.

No.	Date launched	Lifted by	Date raised	Remarks
S49	10.4.15			In shallow water.
S50	24.4.15			In shallow water.
V125	18.5.17			Beached.
V126	30.6.17			Beached and to France.
V127	28.7.17			Beached and to Dordrecht.
V128	11.8.17			To Italy.
S131	3.3.17	Scapa Flow Salvage & Shipbreaking Co.	29.8.24	In shallow water.*
S132	19.5.17			In shallow water – to USA where sunk by gunfire of US battleship *Delaware* and destroyer *Herbert*.

* Three other destroyers which cannot be identified were also raised from shallow water by this company.

No. 7 Flotilla

S56	11.12.15	Cox & Danks	5.6.25	
S65	14.10.16	Cox & Danks	16.5.25	
V78	19.2.16	Cox & Danks	7.9.25	
V83	5.7.16			In shallow water. Recovered by R.N.
G92	15.2.16			Beached.
S136	1.12.17	Cox & Danks	3.4.25	
S137	9.3.18			Beached in shallow water.
S138	22.4.18	Cox & Danks	1.5.25	
H145	14.3.25	Cox & Danks	14.3.25	
G89	11.12.15			Recovered by R.N.

No. 7 (Half) Flotilla

S36	7.10.14	Cox & Danks	18.4.25	
S51	29.4.15			In shallow water.
S52	14.6.15	Cox & Danks	13.10.24	
S60	3.4.16			Beached and to Japan, but later scrapped in UK.
V80	28.4.16			Scuttled but beached and to Japan. Later scrapped in UK.

Bibliography

The Triumph of the Royal Navy by Major Gibbon – Official Record of Surrender Of German Fleet, 1919.

Das Grab der deutscher Flotte by Vice-Admiral L. von Reuter – R.F. Roehler, Leipzig 1921.

Marine Salvage in Peace and War by Commodore T. McKenzie CB, CBE, RN – The Institution of Engineers and Shipbuilders in Scotland, Vol 93, Paper 1122.

Eight Years of Salvage Work at Scapa Flow by E.F. Cox – The Institute of Mechanical Engineers, Proceedings (Fifth Thomas Gray lecture 1932).

The Salving of the Ex-German High Seas Fleet at Scapa Flow by I.D.M. Taylor, SIMechE – The Institution of Mechanical Engineers Scottish Branch – Graduates Section, November 1961.

Ocean Salvage by D. A. Koster (Ch 7) – Gerald Duckworth & Co Ltd, 1971.

Deep Sea Salvage by Whyte and Hadfield – Sampson, Low, Marston & Co.

Deep Sea Diving and Submarine Operations edited by Robert N. Davis – St Catherine Press, 6th edition, 1955.

The Man who Bought a Navy by Gerald Bowman – Harrap & Co, London 1964.

The Story of Scapa Flow by Geoffrey Cousins – Muller & Co, London 1965.

When Ships go Down by David Masters – Eyre & Spottiswoode, 1934.

Encyclopaedia Britannica.

Acknowledgements

To Mr R.W. McCrone MC, for his unstinting help and kindness in providing me with material and contacts without which this account would have been incomplete.

To former staff and employees of the salvage companies concerned who provided me with valuable information, especially Messrs Max Wilkinson, J. Robertson, CEng, FRINA, who also gave me permission to use some of his diagrams, R.R. Drysdale who provided me with some of his working papers, and A.S. Thomson and many others who volunteered memories of the salvage operations.

To Lady Esmé Whistler, Miss A. Parry and Admiral Sir Henry McCall, KCVO, KBE, CB, DSO, for permission to use copyright material relating to the surrender of the German fleet and the subsequent scuttling of the ships.

To the editors of *The Engineer* and *Shipbuilding and Shipping Record* for permission to use material and diagrams in published articles.

To Ian Allan Ltd for permission to use statistics from their publication *German Warships of World War I* by John C. Taylor.

To Norval Ltd for permission to reproduce several photographs.

To Gerald G.A. Meyer, Editor of *The Orcadian,* for help and his permission to draw upon material in past issues of his periodical.

To Mrs I. McKenzie for permission to make use of her own memories of Scapa Flow and of copyright material written by her husband, the late Commodore McKenzie, CB, CBE, RNVR.

To Mr Charles Patterson, MA, CEng, for information, photographs and for permission to make use of his lecture notes and articles on the surrender of the German fleet and salvage operations.

To Mr G. Fleming of Shipbreaking Industries Ltd for the loan of numerous photographs.

To Professor J.M. Peterson, MA for information concerning the early salvage operations.

To Dr R.V. Williams of the British Steel Corporation for information relating to post-1945 steel.

To Mr Steven Hull, BSc for information on skin-diving.

To the editors of *Sea Breezes* and *The Shetland Times* for publicising my requests for information.

To Siebe Gorman & Co Ltd for photographs and permission to use material from *Deep Sea Diving and Submarine Operations* by the late Sir Robert Davis.

The following public bodies have also been most helpful: Hampshire County Library, National Reference Library of Science and Invention, The National Central Library, Public Record Office, The British Museum, The Imperial War Museum, the Institution of Mechanical Engineers and the Ministry of Defence (Naval Historical Branch).

Index